Beatrice

Keep a Steppin'

Beatrice

Keep a Steppin'

Mary Elizabeth Harris

Clovercroft Publishing

Beatrice: Keep a Steppin'

©2019 by Mary Elizabeth Harris

Published by Clovercroft Publishing, Franklin, Tennessee

Scripture taken from THE HOLY BIBLE, NEW INTERNATIONAL VERSION®, NIV® Copyright © 1973, 1978, 1984, 2011 by Biblica, Inc.™ Used by permission. All rights reserved worldwide.

The Authorized (King James) Version of the Bible ('the KJV'), the rights in which are vested in the Crown in the United Kingdom, is reproduced here by permission of the Crown's patentee, Cambridge University Press.

Copyedit by Lapiz Digital Solutions

Cover Design by Omar Mediano

Interior Design by Suzanne Lawing

Printed in the United States of America

978-1-948484-43-5

For Beatrice
who came as temporary caregiver
and stayed ten years as best friend

Contents

Part II: Beatrice

Acknowledgments

"Manuscript? The beginning of a manuscript? Me? Publish? Really?"

In her kind but succinct, bottom-line manner, she answered, "Yes."

"Would you tell me more?"

"Just keep writing. Email me in a few months when you have more, and we'll talk then. Goodbye."

I'd just taken a long breath by completing and turning in my final project for that semester's creative writing class. Dr. Janet Harris, my challenging professor in graduate writing classes, was demanding yet encouraging and her classes informative and engaging. She had just put a carrot in front of me, and I reached but was left to think. I knew my topic was worthy of publishing and began putting my efforts into writing this book. I had stories, interviews, and research to pursue, so I wrote. And I wrote. Then I wrote more.

After graduating with my Master of Liberal Studies degree in creative writing, I spent weeks and months finalizing my manuscript, and Dr. Harris became my editor. Then began my hardest work—revising and revising and revising until I wanted to quit. But I didn't. At times I heard suggestions that were hard to hear, but I listened because I cared about my subject and respected my editor.

Dr. Harris, I deeply appreciate your professionalism, expertise, encouragement, guidance, patience, and support during this process and your belief in me to write Beatrice's story. My wish is that the reader remember Beatrice's example of faith, dealing with hardship, and finding joy in everyday life long after reading her story.

Marvella, Beatrice's younger daughter, was a goldmine whose time, stories, and memory helped weave together threads of her mother's life. Marvella, I still visualize the tiny house in Oak Cliff bulging at the seams with your mama, daddy, and five small children. We've laughed and cried together. Some of your memories were funny, some difficult to hear, but all impactful. I learned about difficult days when school integration began. I am forever grateful for your sweet spirit, immeasurable help, and friendship.

Vera, Beatrice's older daughter, told heartwarming stories about her mother. Vera, do you remember when we spoke, I had to think fast because your phone had limited minutes and would cut off if we exceeded those, and we laughed about that? You quickly settled into your own memories once saying, "Mama was the laughter of the whole family." I heard from you the running theme of your mama's life: resilience—never letting grief or hardship determine her life.

Todd, Beatrice's grandson and Marvella's son, shared memories that imparted wonderful insight into his grandmother as well as showing the deep respect and love he has for her. Todd, the morning we sat and reminisced on the exact pew where your grandmother had sat so many Sundays is a treasured memory. The setting of the lovely, quiet sanctuary of Salem Baptist Church put me closer to Beatrice's story. God had a plan for the little boy Beatrice took to church every Sunday: the boy who played, sang, and ate a donut at Salem—the boy who would one day return as pastor of that same church. Your journey is a beautiful story, and you credit your grandmother for your love of the Lord and your profession.

Patrice, Beatrice's first grandchild and Vera's daughter, helped me learn about her brother, Rashad. Patrice, I learned from your time caring for my mother how close you and Beatrice were. As we spoke, I heard the pain of seeing your beloved grandmother, who had influenced you so much, slip into the winter of her life.

Kyisha, Beatrice's great-granddaughter and Patrice's daughter, was just what I expected. 'Isha, I'd heard stories for years from your great-grandmother about the escapades you two shared, and I love that you are Beatrice's "mini-me." You recalled so easily the strength and encouragement she gave you your whole life, especially when college was hard.

From Nicy, Beatrice's niece, I heard the incredible history of the farm in Clarksville. Nicy, your information made the story of the Dilworth family a deeper and more important story, educating me and therefore readers of the historical background of Beatrice's family after Abraham Lincoln signed the Emancipation Proclamation and what life was like for black farmers in the South in the 1930s and 1940s. Thank you for your time and sharing.

From Day One in graduate school at SMU, Dr. Dianne Goode genuinely supported and encouraged my writing in her six art history classes, two of those in Italy and France. Dianne, little did we know that the spark you helped reignite in me for learning and writing would culminate in this book. Proof of this spark was the joy I experienced the night I sat on the floor in the Hamon Library, pulling books from the shelves and discovering Matisse's motif of the open window in his painting. Dianne, I value your gift of teaching and continued support but most of all your friendship.

"Professa," Dr. Njoki McElroy, you gave me first-hand knowledge of growing up in the same years and area of Texas as Beatrice, educated me on the closeness of black communities, and shared how it was for you growing up in a segregated society. Assigning me the role of "Madea" in our class production was akin to being assigned to play Beatrice and was so much fun, but I gained insight from having to see life from the eyes of a black grandmother. Dr. McElroy, you and Beatrice are mirror images of strength and perseverance.

Thanks to Dianne Peek of the Clarksville Chamber of Commerce who directed me to Danielle Petty, Director of the Red River County Public Library. Danielle, your research for information on Ophelia and Searcey Dilworth resulted in finding the obituary of Ophelia. From that, I gained greater insight into the loving, hardworking Dilworth family of the 1930s and 1940s in Clarksville.

Jim Clark, after researching the history of Clarksville, I was delighted to talk to you about the namesake and ancestor of the first Jim Clark who founded the town in the early 1830s. We had a connection because you knew Beatrice and her mother, which was amazing. You told me about Haywood, the black section of Clarksville, where Beatrice and her family lived and where she grew up. Thank you for your time.

I am grateful to my daughters, Jenny Harris Crandall and Sally Harris Falwell, for your memories and insight into Beatrice and to my sons, Virgil and Dan, for your support in this endeavor of mine. Thank you Evey, my granddaughter, and Sally for consulting with me on Beatrice's book cover.

I am grateful to Jack Brown, Fran Jackson, and Julie Cochran for your time, memories and stories of Beatrice, and for the friendship we share.

My "Dark and Stormy Writing Group" was a continual source of thoughtful feedback, encouragement, and support. Thank you Bonnie, Mary G., Sarette, Pam, Liz, Sean, Johnnie, and Laura. You fostered growth, creativity, laughter, and friendship throughout Beatrice's story.

I thank my patient and supportive Monday bridge group for tolerating my erratic attendance, so I could write: Beverly, Boo, Carol, Drew, Jane, Joan, both Julies, Lynn, Mary, Patsy, and Sally. I loved the Monday you let me walk in on your serious, high-scoring games to offer readers' opinions when I needed them.

Thank you Danny, Martha, Marilyn, Linda, Susan, Sally, Carolyn and Lawrence, Lynda and Harris, and Debra and Rick for your continued love and support throughout my life and especially in my endeavor to write Beatrice's story. Each of you knew Beatrice and loved her too.

Thank you, Beatrice, for your wisdom to always "keep a steppin'."

Author's Note

Beatrice, you are the one who wrote your story. I just put it on paper. You gave me the stories and memories with which I began writing about you a long time ago. We shared so many memories and stories together from when you nursed me after back surgery to the day-after-day, year-after-year caring for my mother. That nine years with Mom was a trip, wasn't it? We laughed; shared stories of pain, joy, and sorrows; and without words respected, loved, and trusted each other. All three of us. From you, I learned to talk straight. How did you always have an answer for everything and insights that simplified what the world can make so complicated? Your simple wisdom in dealing with injustice, unfairness, pain, people that drive us crazy, and even death often made me laugh, but more importantly, made me think. Your words of strength and wisdom are ones I'll always remember.

You helped make what could have been challenging days caring for my mother not so challenging. Your sense of humor was a rare gem, and your infectious laugh made life lighter. As Mom and all your patients said, you gave the best bed bath of anyone. B, your Christian faith, love for your family, devotion to Salem Baptist, compassion for the sick and elderly, generosity to anyone in need, and ability to make mundane events into a funny story were unique gifts that meant so much to so many. Beatrice stories will always be told. I've told some as my loving tribute.

B, this tribute to you is based on years of my memories and our stories as well as stories from your family and patients' families for whom you worked. If I have inadvertently mis-recalled or misinterpreted, please know all has been written with love and gratitude.

Part I: The Nurse

1

Ice Chips

There she stood. White against black. I briefly opened my eyes and saw her. Who was she? I didn't know or care. What I did know was that I felt paralyzing pain. I heard noise through my fog—too much noise. She stood quietly back, away from the people in white uniforms and others with just white skin. I saw her through my groggy pain. Black against white.

I was in the hospital and had survived a critical back surgery. The nurses in their crisp white uniforms thought I needed to sit up and then stand. How stupid; I was in excruciating pain lying still. The quiet woman standing in the back wouldn't have done that. I moaned in pain, they kept on, and I fainted. Thank goodness.

My loving mother understood the critical nature of my surgery and the difficulty of recovery. I did not. My mother wanted me to have constant care, more than overworked nurses could provide. A nurse for two weeks was her offer of a birthday present for me. I declined her offer. I did not want someone looking over me every second, plus the hospital had nurses. Thank goodness wisdom trumped arrogance. My wise mother ignored me and called a friend of mine who gave her the phone number of a nurse. Mother spoke with the nurse on the phone and hired her without my knowing. Enter Beatrice Jones. She was the solitary black against white.

Finally in a room, there was peace. I hurt so much I could neither move nor talk. If I moaned, there she was by my bed with cool ice chips for a parched mouth. She knew; she just knew what to do. No words.

The third day, however, Beatrice took charge, and I mean took charge. "It is time for a bath." I weakly protested as she prepared a tub of warm water, a washcloth, and soap. She moved quietly and began the process I feared because there was pain each time I moved, even slightly.

I was surprised. Beatrice knew every move to make so I didn't hurt. The warm water felt good. She covered my skin so I didn't get cold. She worked quickly, and my bath was over before I knew it. She rubbed fresh-smelling lotion and put a clean gown on me. She laid my head back gently on the pillow and brushed my hair. It felt so good to be clean, and I'll never forget how good Beatrice's brushing my hair felt. She was doing for me what I could not do for myself.

I began to get the picture. I was in charge of nothing. Doctors, nurses, and Beatrice were in charge of everything. First it was the bath; then I was told I needed to eat. "I'm not hungry."

"Well, you need to eat," she said as she put spoonfuls of scrambled eggs or mashed potatoes to my mouth. I had no choice with this nurse. Finally I would turn my head. I'd eaten a few bites, and Beatrice was satisfied. Then I'd rest.

Beatrice was quiet, and I realized she would not be the kind of nurse who wanted to talk all the time. If I moaned "ice," she was right there. When my mother would come, I could hear them whispering together. As my mother lovingly held my arm and caressed my hair, I could see the relief in her eyes that Beatrice Jones was caring for her little girl. I was 46.

As I began to feel better, I felt glad to see Beatrice walk in the door at 8:00 a.m. each morning. She'd ask how I was and go down the hall for coffee. We'd go through our routine, doctors would come by, and she would report anything of significance. The doctors realized Beatrice knew her work.

The third day, my kind surgeon came in and asked how I was. Referring to nurses and physical therapists who would turn me to check on drainage tubes and force me to sit up while every move was painful, I honestly told him, "They're trying to kill me." I could hear the funniest little chuckle from where Beatrice was sitting as the doctor reassured me he would not let that happen.

One of my crazy friends brought me a gag gift of a typical, orange medicine bottle with a fake prescription for laughter taped on the side. The bottle and typed prescription looked real. When opened, however, this bottle emitted peals of laughter. The prescription said to take this medicine three times a day.

I could barely smile at my gift at this point. But the next day, for the first time, I felt as if I might live. Another surgeon came in later that morning and asked if I was about ready to go home. Was he crazy? I'd just graduated from a bedpan to the bathroom; I couldn't even sit up in bed or walk to the bathroom without Beatrice, a nurse, or physical therapist. I didn't know how best to respond to this doctor with an emphatic "no," so I picked up my new medicine bottle, held it toward him, and opened it. Laughter pealed forth. The always unsmiling doctor smiled, and then laughed himself. "I guess that's a no."

This occasion gave me information about this nurse my mother had hired. When I opened the laughing medicine bottle to answer the doctor, Beatrice didn't chuckle. She giggled out loud in surprise. I learned this woman had a sense of humor.

At dusk that Friday afternoon, after dinner, I realized I was feeling better. It had been a difficult week, but now I had a little relief from the fear and pain. Beatrice came and sat in a chair by my bed, and I smiled at her. We talked a little, and then I asked her to turn on the TV. Up until now, I'd wanted no noise at all. *Matlock* was just beginning. The room was dark and quiet except for the light from the television. I will always treasure the sweet memory of Beatrice and me quietly watching *Matlock* together, her chair by my bed, and lights from the city flickering outside my hospital window. Even today, 25 years later, I watch *Matlock* reruns because of the sweet memory of pain subsiding while knowing I had the companionship of someone by my side who would help me get through this ordeal. Beatrice Jones was becoming my friend.

Once at home and on a walker, I was relieved Beatrice would be at home with me. I was tentatively walking even on a walker and terrified to shower. She would help me up on the walker, grab a piece of the back of my gown, and slowly walk beside me to the bathroom. "All right, Mary, sit down here, and I'll help you with your gown. I've already got the water on, and it's nice and warm. You take my arm right here and step into the tub."

"Hold onto me, Beatrice. I'm afraid I'll slip."

"No, you won't. You're just fine, and I'm right here. I'll wash your back and legs, and you just stand there in that warm water as long as you want to." The warm water did feel good, and when I was ready, Beatrice would slowly help me out, wrap a towel around me, and help me sit while she rubbed lotion on me. She'd slip a fresh gown over my head; I'd brush my teeth and then make the slow walk back to bed. Beatrice had clean sheets on my bed. A shower and clean sheets felt wonderful. While I slept, she would do the wash. These were sweet days of slowly getting better with a reassuring helper by my side.

Beatrice would do anything I asked. She'd "fry up a chicken," my favorite. As cabin fever began to engulf me, Beatrice would help me in her car, and we'd drive to La Madeleine's each morning, have tea, and talk. By now, I was able to walk tentatively without a walker.

I'd ask her to stop at the Southern Methodist University (SMU) track on the way home so I could walk. I was supposed to walk, and it felt good to be outside. I was unsure and slow at first but improved. In two or three weeks, I was able to walk a little faster than Beatrice wanted to walk, and she would just chuckle and then mimic my walk. We laughed together a lot. Being out walking was a great confidence booster. We then went home, ate lunch, and talked a bit. I would nap, and Beatrice would go home.

By this time, I knew from some of Beatrice's stories that she was often called "B" and sometimes "Be-AT" by neighbors and friends at church. She had become my supportive companion, so she became "B" to me. My children got to know B well, too, and loved her immediately. They were busy with school and sports, and my husband was busy with work and golf. My mother would come by to visit and always knew not to stay too long. As I look back, I realize Beatrice gave my mother as much comfort as she gave me. Beatrice Jones and I got to know each other over these few weeks.

When it was time for B to leave, I wasn't sad because I was getting better and managing on my own. Healing was slow. The doctor had said it would take a year for full recovery. I was fastidious in following all postsurgical instructions. The back brace I wore, more like a corset from earlier centuries, only came off when I showered, and I began to think of the brace as my friend for six months. The nurses and physical therapists helped me learn how to put my "corset" on with minimal pain, and once at home, B would help. Soon the back brace became a natural part of my clothing.

Two months after B left, my family was at the airport, flying to be at my son's graduation ceremony. Security was immediately alerted because of all the metal around my torso. I was thoroughly checked as I stood spread-eagled against a wall, just like any felon. B got so tickled when I told her about this incident, and I realized then how special it was to have someone who had shared my pain and fear and now shared my recovery. Beatrice Jones was a huge part of my healing and regaining a normal life.

Keep a Steppin' is the story of how Beatrice became part of my life, my mother's life, and my family's life. I didn't realize it then, but a wonderful person had begun to weave herself into the fabric of our lives. I wouldn't fully appreciate this for seven more years.

Beatrice and I kept up on the phone for a few weeks. Then the conversations became further apart and soon stopped. B was with a new patient, and I began driving carpools and taking kids to soccer again. I was so grateful to be doing these mundane things once more.

Two years later, the phone rang. It was Beatrice. She'd had car trouble not too far away and needed help. I was happy to hear from her and glad to assist. I felt pleased that she would call me. For twenty years, she never forgot that afternoon and "what I did." To help her was such a little thing, but her gratitude for my being able to give back to her was mentioned off and on for years. Beatrice Jones and I were friends.

2

"Yea Though We Walk..."

On a cold Tuesday night at 11:30, the call came. Through sleep, I heard a strange voice say, "Your mother has just been rushed to the hospital." My heart was pounding as I quickly dressed. I was terrified. I didn't even know if she was alive as I raced to the hospital. Mother had been irritable on the phone that morning, and later I was to understand why. My last words with her had been abrupt.

Three days earlier, late on Saturday night, Mother had fallen and hit her head on a sharp corner of her chest of drawers. She was 89. When I arrived at her apartment, I was shocked. Mother looked as if she'd been in a car accident. Her left eye was blackened and cut, and the entire left side of her face was red from abrasions. There was a pool of blood on the carpet where she'd fallen.

Stitches repaired the largest cut, and the CAT scan was clear. Mom stayed with us over the weekend, resting and visiting when she felt like it. By Monday morning, she felt much better and wanted to go home. All this time, however, blood had slowly been seeping into her brain.

At 2:00 a.m., the surgeon came in the small emergency room and told my 16-year-old son and me, "The CAT scan shows a subdural hematoma that will require immediate brain surgery. I cannot operate until the Coumadin is out of her system, and I do not expect your mother to live that long." Dan and I were blindsided upon hearing the doctor's blunt neurological assessment. How could this be? Mother was chatty and laughing just two days before. As I looked down at my unconscious mother and Dan at his grandmother, he and I fell sobbing into each other's arms. Earlier I had declined my son's offer to go with me to the hospital, but he followed me anyway. Dan was there for me at a devastating time.

After Mother was in triage for five hours, the Coumadin had been drained from her system, she was still alive, and she was wheeled into surgery. She was not expected to survive the surgery. She did. She had only a 10 percent chance of living once she was in the intensive care unit (ICU), and if she did, the extent of brain damage would not be known for weeks, even months. Severe brain damage was a real possibility. This was a terrible reality to live with.

Mother survived. After months of ups and downs, hospitals, recovery, and physical therapy, she was released to live in an assisted living facility. Ten months after that frightening phone call, my mother was playing the piano and bridge at Caruth Haven.

Waiting for days to watch a loved one unexpectedly teeter between life and death results in an exhaustion and fear that defies description. The ICU became my home. My schedule became hospital and home, home and hospital. The uncertainty was draining. How long could I go on like this? I was desperate for relief and had only one idea.

I dialed a familiar number. "Hi, B, this is Mary."

"I know who it is." B always said that when I called. I told her the story about Mother.

"B, is there any way you could relieve me for a few afternoons in the hospital?" She explained she had a job caring for an elderly man every other week but could help on the weeks she was off. When B walked into the waiting room the following afternoon, never in my life had I been so relieved and happy to see someone.

Beatrice Jones was always calm. She understood illness and had witnessed illness and death her entire life, personally and professionally. Nothing ruffled her. The day-to-day and month-to-month recovery from Mother's brain surgery was miraculous, yet it was slow, uncertain, and arduous. I was able to stay sane because of the relief, support, confidence, humor, and love Beatrice Jones brought into the sterile hospital rooms while my mother lay unresponsive for weeks.

Nurses told me talking to my mother as much as possible was the best thing I could do for her. I talked and talked. I brought my daughter's wedding album full of family pictures that were reminders of a wonderfully happy time a mere three months before. Although unresponsive, Mother's soft brown eyes would settle on the pictures, day after day, as I would turn the pages—as if her brain were somehow trying to connect to what she saw. But there was no response. B showed her the pictures when she was there.

One day as I lay by my mother's side in her hospital bed and again turned the pages of the wedding album, I was surprised by what I thought was a small spark of recognition in her eyes. She was gazing at a picture of herself and me and slowly raised her hand, pointed with her little arthritic finger, and said her first unsure but clear words, "That's sweet." I was stunned. My eyes got big, and I looked at my tenacious mother. I had just been privileged to witness an atrophied, 89-year-old brain show recognition for the first time in weeks following the trauma of severe hemorrhage and brain surgery. I couldn't wait to tell B. That moment was thrilling and gave the first sign of hope. "That's sweet" are two words I'll never forget. They put a joy in my heart I hadn't felt in a long time and bound a mother and daughter ever closer.

I kept on talking. Even Beatrice said she couldn't outtalk me. Talking and turning on *Wheel of Fortune* without sound was all I knew to do. At home, Mother had always watched that TV show. I was helpless, otherwise, to help my mother recover. While Mom slept, B and I would talk softly, just as she and my mother had talked softly when I was in the hospital.

I'd lie in Mother's bed with her. I was tired of the chair by the bed and later came to believe the physical closeness was emotionally healing for both of us. On this particular day, I'd brought some hand lotion, and I smoothed it on her hands as we lay side by side. Mother slowly lifted her arms, lotion dripping down her hands, down her arms, and onto the sheets. She was blank, having no idea what to do. Her brain could not process this simple act of rubbing lotion on her hands, something she'd done a million times. I was saddened, but B would not let me stay that way. She reminded me of the photograph recognition and the doctor saying every day would be up and down with a brain injury. Beatrice Jones accepted each day with whatever it brought. If things were good, that's fine. If not, they would be soon. "Just keep movin'."

Yes, there was always uncertainty and heaviness with which to deal, and hopes for recovery were constantly dashed. Beatrice brought a steadiness and calmness that helped me immeasurably. There were little things we chuckled at together, and there were times when we just sat quietly by Mom's bed.

I knew friends at church who would read Scripture to critically ill family members for comfort. That was something else I could do. I brought my Bible to Mom's room early one evening and turned to the 23rd Psalm while standing by her bed. I began, "The Lord is my Shepherd; I shall not want. He makes me lie down in green pastures, he leads me beside still waters, he restores my soul. . . . Yea, though I walk through the valley of the shadow of death, I will fear no evil, for Thou art . . . ."

"Stop that!" B, standing by the window, looked over at me as she issued her command. "No more 'yea though we walk!' Child, quit readin' all about death to your mother. You're gonna have her in the grave before she's ready to get there!" This was the most unexpected interruption I've ever experienced.

My friend Anne had come to see Mother and me that night, and we were both totally caught off guard with Beatrice's command. We started laughing and then could not stop. Here's this devout Christian woman telling me, in no uncertain terms, to quit reading the Bible to my ill mother. What was Beatrice Jones going to say next?

After B's mandate, I put my Bible aside, still surprised, and changed directions. "Mom, you have the prettiest brown eyes." She looked up at me and smiled. She had not smiled at the 23rd Psalm and my attempt at spiritual solace. Beatrice came out with these quips that were direct, unexpected, and stated with such certainty that anyone would listen. I treasured her brand of wisdom. She knew. She just knew what was appropriate for her patients and for my mother.

Anne remembers that incident to this day and occasionally brings it up. We look at each other and visualize the hospital room, the darkness outside, and B instructing me to "stop that!" Anne then fills in with the rest of B's classic statement: "Mary, no more 'yea though we walk!'" Once again, we laugh until we can't even talk, and Anne has tears running down her cheeks from laughing so hard which makes me laugh even harder.

Soon after the debacle of the 23rd Psalm, Mother was transferred to the Jackson Building, a rehabilitation hospital in the Presbyterian Hospital complex. She'd gone from days in the ICU to a hospital room and now the Jackson Building.

During these hospital transitions, Beatrice was there every step of the way. These were long and worrisome days, but I had a companion to talk to about my mother, one who gave perspective on uncertainty and waiting—and one who did not leave my mother's side. While Mother was in the Jackson Building, B would come in every morning at 9:00. Mother would often look at her and complain, "You're late." B was wonderful because no complaint, criticism, or odd behavior ever got her upset, but she always did have a reply.

In this case, after hearing "you're late," B would respond to Mom, "Mrs. Tompkins, look at that big ole clock up there. See, it says 9:00. I'm right on time." Mother would glare at B. On some level, my mother knew enough now to understand something was severely wrong with her. She was no longer in control of her life, and she was angry. Although she didn't have a response to Beatrice, my mother would make the same complaint the next day and the next, and B's response was always the same. This interchange was Mom's and Beatrice's morning greeting to each other for several weeks.

Beatrice always spoke to her patients as if they were in a normal conversation, not as if they were old or there was something wrong with them. She did not judge. She had the compassion to accept those for whom she worked, no matter the mood or behavior, but B always had an answer as she did with my mother's complaints about being late. Beatrice Jones took everything in stride, and that allowed her sense of humor to balance difficult days. Eventually this trait also helped my mother sometimes laugh at herself as the months and years passed.

My mother complained daily about the nurses in the Jackson Building. The nurses would often get her up in the night because my mother, a high fall risk, would unthinkingly try to get out of bed. Instead of restraining her, they chose to put her in a wheelchair and take her to sit at the nurses' station. They knew my mother loved the piano, so they would place her wheelchair at the piano nearby and ask her to play.

The way it got translated to B the following mornings was, "They did it again. They wake me up at 3:00 in the morning and make me entertain them. Get me out of here! I hate this place!"

Mother did hate the Jackson Building. She was scared and angry because she could not process what was going on in her injured brain. To see my placid mother upset made me sad. The way B would tell events of the day to me, though, often made me laugh and dispelled fatigue and sadness.

One morning, Mother wasn't in her room, so I walked to the living area. She was seated in her wheelchair, and I smiled as I saw her before she saw me. She looked pretty and serene. My mother was a Southern lady who spoke thoughtfully and quietly. She was gentle. I am sure I never heard her use slang. As she saw me that morning, I bent over and said, "Hi, Mom." I'll never forget her response.

"What'd ya know, Joe?" What did she just say? Where in the world did that come from? To say I was surprised is an understatement. I never heard a statement more out of character from my mother as well as the flippant way she said, "What'd ya know, Joe?" She looked at me, pleased with herself for conversing as if all was normal. I smiled big and had no idea how to respond. I took hold of her hands and looked into the eyes of a very brave woman. When I told B that story, she loved it. For a while, I kept a journal of things my mother said. A brain waking up from severe injury is fascinating—and sometimes funny.

There were many days when things did not go well. When B was not available, she sent her granddaughter, Patrice, who was in nursing school at El Centro. I was unsure about another person dealing with my mother, but if Beatrice thought Patrice would be fine, I did too. As soon as I met Patrice, I liked her. Beatrice's mother's legacy of nursing the sick was continuing, now to four generations. Patrice was a lot like B—responsible, smart, and kind, yet she was quiet, unlike her grandmother. I felt better with Beatrice and Patrice than I did with some of the nurses.

After a difficult six weeks at the Jackson Building, Mother was transferred to skilled nursing at the Forum for more rehabilitation, physical therapy, and extended care. She was still so sick. Adjustment to skilled nursing was difficult and discouraging. This journey, since the late-night emergency call, had once seemed interminable but became my new normal. I'd quit counting the days, weeks, and months, and I was not so overwhelmed, thanks to Beatrice and Patrice, who made the waiting not so heavy and lonely.

With her feeding tube out, Mother was put on pureed food to redevelop her swallowing reflex. Choking was a real danger. Patients on pureed food sat at a long table that faced the back wall. Seeing Mom sitting here was sad and depressing, and after tasting her pureed carrots, I knew why she had zero interest in eating. B and I tried to encourage Mom to eat, to no avail.

One day Jenny, my daughter, came to visit her grandmother at the Forum. Mom, B, Jenny, and I sat in four upright chairs that B had pulled together so we could talk. I can still see us sitting in what appeared a stiff, uncomfortable grouping to visit, but this was a hospital room. Jenny and her grandmother often had fairly direct conversations, and Jenny was aware of our nutritional concern for Mother, who refused to eat that awful, pureed food. After chatting for a few minutes about school, Jenny looked at her grandmother and said, "Mama T, you need to eat more."

As quickly as Jenny said, "Mama T, you need to eat more," my mother, calm but unsmiling, looked right at Jenny, "You eat less." Jenny, a freshman at Texas Christian University (TCU), had gained the expected "freshman 15." Jenny, B, and I were stunned not only that Mom was talking, but that she had responded rationally. Maybe not appropriately, to say the least, but rationally. That was huge. As Beatrice heard my mother's response to Jenny, she stifled her laugh and had to get up from her stiff chair and walk around before she was able to collect herself.

At first, Jenny was caught off guard at the blunt, unsolicited advice from her brain-injured, elderly grandmother but then laughed, happy to hear the grandmother she loved make a rational, although embarrassing, response in a conversation. Jenny and Mama T had a close relationship, and they both had always tried to help the other. What a day.

Mother still had days of ups and downs, but the downs were less intense. She did everything Jarrod, the physical therapist, asked of her. B and I would sit outside the therapy room and watch through the glass. We would chat and watch Mother and Jarrod throw a giant orange rubber exercise ball back and forth. It didn't matter they sat only two feet apart. What did matter was that Mom's brain was sending the message to her hands to catch the ball. B would get tickled at her, and I thought my mother looked so cute proudly catching that giant rubber ball at age 90. Mom was an engaged patient for Jarrod, and Jarrod was a dedicated physical therapist and encourager.

Those two spent days walking the halls with Beatrice following. B would chuckle and tell me how pleased Mom would be when Jarrod praised her progress. My mother was beginning to have cognition, purpose to her days, and slow but sure progress.

3

A New Dress Every Day

To get to know a person takes time. I've been taken aback from time to time by changes or outbursts in someone's behavior, which can alter a relationship. Beatrice Jones was who she was, day in and day out. This unique woman had become such a part of our family that I wondered where she'd been all my life.

She could talk your ear off, or she could be quiet. She was trustworthy. She was spunky, dependable, unflappable. She had the most infectious laugh I've ever heard, a solution to any problem, a wonderful sense of humor, and a respect for all people, including herself. Beatrice was strong, confident, and compassionate, so much so that she handled the oddest and crankiest people and situations with seeming ease. B never felt sorry for herself because that was being in "the pit, and no one's puttin' me there!"

Beatrice's work ethic was impeccable. To her, having a job was all about self-respect, responsibility, and character. A job mowing yards was as respectable as president of the United States. She would say, "He has a job, doesn't matter what it is." Her son-in-law has been on the Dallas City Council for years and was mayor pro tem for a while. I asked B why she never told me about Tennell being mayor pro tem because being mayor when the actual mayor is gone is a big deal. Her reply never changes, "He has a job." That's all she said. Beatrice Jones had never been impressed by wealth or status. Not one bit. She looked at who people were, not what they had.

Beatrice Jones was the most real example of a Christian I have ever known. She had loved and been devoted to her church, Salem Baptist, and was there every time the doors opened. When I would be sad, she would say, "Don't you worry. The Lord's in charge and knows what's best."

When a friend's three-month-old baby tragically died of SIDS, I was heartbroken and asked why God would allow that. I had held that friend's baby in my arms. B's thoughtful response to me reflected her core beliefs: "This is very sad. I'm sad for those parents. But, Mary, babies are His children. We can't see what would have happened to that baby in the years to come. Later on, something could have happened. I can see only down this hall. We can't see all the way down the road, and He can. We all have an appointed time. None of us is here to stay. Get that in your head. And if you've got a nice place to move to, you don't mind moving.

"Mary, we've made so much out of dying, and we've never done it, so we don't know. We don't want anybody to die. . . . Well, there's a few, we might want 'em to stay dead for a while, but then we'd go wake 'em up. If it's gonna be for me to have a bad stroke, then that's what I'll die from. We don't know what it'll be. The Lord is with me, and He's with Baby Henry." I was silent. I had listened, and Beatrice's unwavering belief in God's all-knowing love and compassion comforted me.

Beatrice's deep faith was unshakable. This is the reason she was able to accept the blows that occurred in her life, and there were terrible blows. What molded a young black girl raised in the Jim Crow era to have her strength and wisdom, compassion and love?

To answer this question, Beatrice's story takes us back to a small sharecropper's farm in Clarksville, Texas, in the 1930s and 1940s where she grew up. Poverty was all her family knew during those years. Her father farmed the portion of land allotted to him, and her mother worked as a maid, babysitter, and caregiver for white folks in Clarksville. With hardworking, Christian parents who were strong role models, four sisters, and three brothers, Beatrice grew up with a foundation of hard work and family. Life was difficult, but the core of the woman she was to become developed during these years.

Bathing in a metal tub once a week, especially in winter, most likely was the reason Beatrice appreciated warm water. One cold Dallas morning, she came into work and as she pulled off her coat said, "Oh, I say every morning in the shower, 'Lord, thank you for this warm water.'" She said this with feeling, and I knew she was truly grateful. I'd never given much thought to warm water before.

I doubt if Beatrice ever knew, but her one statement that morning about warm water made an impression on me. Recently, as I've pondered the life of Beatrice Dilworth Jones, there are days when I stand in my own shower on cold days, warm water cascading over me, and I'm reminded to say, "Lord, thank you for this warm water." I think of her. Hardship and poverty gave Beatrice a gift of strength to accept difficult situations throughout her life. Those difficulties gave her the gift of gratitude for simple things in life that most take for granted.

Beatrice once told me about a woman in her neighborhood who complained about not having enough. B's response to her friend was a story from her own childhood during years of the Great Depression when her family barely had enough to eat. She told her friend, "I had just one dress to wear to school. If you have just one dress to wear like I did, all you have to do is make sure it's clean and ironed, and you'll be just fine! It'll be like a new dress every day." That one story of Beatrice, the little girl, tells much about who she was throughout her life.

When Beatrice spoke about her childhood in Clarksville, there was never a mention of the poverty nor the blatant racism with which she grew up. She would chuckle as she remembered riding in her father's hay wagon, the "whoppins" she got, and the life she had growing up with her brothers and sisters. When asked if going to a black school apart from white children ever bothered her, she replied, "No, I liked my school. We played with white children after school some, but on weekends, they were with their families and went to their churches, and we were with our families and went to our church." That was just the way it was in the 1930s and 1940s in Clarksville and the South, and it was just fine with B. She was loved and secure in her home.

The Dilworth family name originated from a slave owner in Mississippi who had released Beatrice's great-great-grand-father in 1865 when the Emancipation Proclamation was signed by Abraham Lincoln. Seventy years later, sharecrop-pers, like her father, still had no education and little or no money left over each month after crops paid for taxes and food.

I wanted to know more about Beatrice's childhood on the farm and her adult years, the years before I met her in 1993.

4

For Sale

A t 1544 Gillette, in South Dallas, stood the proud home of Beatrice Dilworth Jones. Four years ago when I went for a visit with Beatrice, I arrived to see a "For Sale" sign in front of her home. I sat in the car and felt a deep sadness. How could this home be for sale? Beatrice loved her home and had taken wonderful care of it. The kitchen was always clean, beds were made, and each room was neat as a pin, no matter how many people were there. There had always been flowers in her flower bed and grass cut in summer. Now Beatrice was in her 80s and ill.

This proud home was full of my mother's furniture that my brother and I gave to Beatrice when Mother died. When we offered the furniture to her, she'd said, "Yes, I'll take it all." She was happy and forever appreciative. There was no one we wanted to have Mother's things more than the woman who had so faithfully and lovingly cared for her day after day.

I knocked, and B's daughter, Vera, answered. I walked in

and looked around at the familiarity of Mother's piano and furniture. I felt proud and happy because everything was spic 'n span and cared for. B had always kept her house clean, and now Vera did that for her. I looked carefully at the family pictures neatly hung in the hall as Vera took me back to B's room. I'd visited B in her home before, but now the reality of her aging struck hard.

Beatrice was ensconced in my mother's blue recliner, which has its own well-known story. Now was the time for B to rest in that famous chair. I smiled a sad smile at the circle of life that changes bring. I hugged B. She was not a hugger and never hesitated to tell me, but I didn't care. I was so glad to see her, I couldn't help myself, and she didn't care a bit. She just laughed. Laughter was B's usual greeting to me whether coming by to see Mom, on the phone, or even in her own home. Almost always. Once I asked her why she laughed when she saw me, and she answered. "You're funny." I hadn't done anything, hadn't had time to even say hi before she'd start chuckling.

Beatrice looked older. She'd always been up and busy in her home before but not now.

We talked for a few minutes, and she pointed to a picture of President Obama on her wall. "That's my boyfriend." I expected this comment because she had said that many times since he became president. I remembered when I took Mother and B to vote in 2008. We got special status because of handicap needs. This was a fun adventure, and the three of us had a jolly time as Mother and B canceled out each other's vote.

I had told B on the phone I wanted to interview her for a college paper I was writing about her. Her instant reply was, "Well, all right, but I wanna see that paper before you turn it in!" Typical. Always an answer. This sunny afternoon I asked if I could record her on my phone. She agreed. The truth is I always wanted to have a memory of B's voice and infectious laugh.

I had to remember that when asked direct questions, B gave short, direct answers. That did not change. I had hoped for more color and details, even just a hint of resentment to the secondary status of blacks she lived with for so many years. That would have made my manuscript more colorful but did not happen.

Knowing she was born in 1930, I asked her, anyway, to ease myself into this interview process.

"B, where were you born?"

"I was born in Clarksville, Texas."

"When were you born?" Now here's the real B.

"Oh, shit, I don't know when."

"Well, B, was it 1930 or 1940?" I didn't want to make her older than she was.

"Yeah, some time like that. I'm 84, so if you can't figure it out, just go ahead and make up something."

"Do you remember growing up in Clarksville?"

"I remember everything about Clarksville."

"What specifically?"

"I remember going to school every day. Second grade . . . don't seem to remember too much about first grade."

"What do you remember about school?"

"Mother made sure we went to school every day because, see, Mother worked at the school for a long time, and she would take us to school every day. She cared a lot about education. She'd usually be home when we got home, but sometimes she'd come back and get us, you know, when we was itty bitty children."

"Did you go to school all year, or did you have to leave at times to help on the farm?"

"Oh, they saw we finished the school year. Now sometimes, the boys had to help on the farm."

"What did your mom do?"

"Mother used to work looking mostly after sick people."

"So, B, is that why you wanted to be a nurse?"

"Yes, that's why I got into nursing—because my mother did that."

"Your dad?"

"He was a farmer"

"What did he grow?"

"What'd he grow?" She found my question amusing for some reason. "Well, he grew everything. He had his own corn, cotton, and all that stuff. He owned his own land."

"At what point did you start in nursing?"

"I went to see Madge, my sister, in Amarillo. We'd go up in summer at times to help with her children. I went up there when I finished school because I couldn't get a job making any money in Clarksville. Yes, I went to school there."

"What was your first job?"

"Amarillo in a nursing home."

This interview was going fast, too fast. No elaboration, no details. I wanted some meat. It was time to broach the subject of segregation. I was a little uncomfortable but then remembered this was an official interview, plus nothing ever shocked B.

"B, what was the difference between blacks and whites growing up?"

"Oh, shit, I don't know. I never paid 'em that much attention."

"Were white people ever mean?"

"No, they wasn't mean. But, see, we didn't associate with 'em much, say, as . . . ."

"What about black and white schools?"

"Oh yeah, those kids went to school not too far from where we went to school."

"So yours was a black school?"

"It was a black school."

"Did that bother you?"

"No. Well, it never bothered me . . . . See, I was never used to white schools."

"Did your parents ever say anything about the separation of blacks from whites?"

"Never heard 'em."

That ended the official interview. It went as expected, with Beatrice's typical short answers. I felt some success. We began talking easily, and that's when I learned more. She began reminiscing as she looked out the window, picturing her family on the farm a lifetime ago.

"Even as a little kid, I was big. I was big, but I was quiet. It confused people because it seems they thought being big meant you talk a lot, and if you're a small kid, you're quiet. Don't know why, but they'd always ask my mama why I was so quiet. Even say to me, 'Don't you ever talk, Boy?' I'd just shrug my shoulders. It didn't really bother me 'cuz my brothers and sisters talked for me, and it didn't ever bother Mama or Daddy. I guess I was just born that way 'cuz Mama always said, 'Curtis, God makes us the way He makes us. Some talk, some don't. Some big, some small.'"

"I was strong too. Guess working in corn fields and pickin' cotton made me strong. But I never liked to fight like my brothers. Yes, I was big, I was strong, but I just didn't like fightin'. One day when my brothers were beatin' up on me, my daddy called me inside and told me if I didn't fight back, he was gonna whip me. I sure 'nough knew I didn't want a whippin'. But I don't remember if I went out and fought 'em."

My interview did not give me any big surprises, but I felt good because I'd seen and visited with B, and I'd gotten her voice and words of growing up in Clarksville. B had always succinctly spoken her mind when it involved direct questions. Conversationally, she could talk and talk and talk. I asked questions that were important to my learning more about her childhood. My questions dealt with life in a small Texas town in the 1930s, her family, school, work, and social life. It was a hard but routine life with her family at the center.

Beatrice often chuckled as she remembered her childhood on the farm in Clarksville. Family memories would first get her tickled, then laughing hard as she would remember. I soon broached a question I didn't want to ask but one which was important. "B, I don't want to ask this next question."

"Just ask it. Go on."

"B, did anyone ever call you the 'N' word?" My question didn't surprise or bother her one bit, but her wise answer surprised me.

"Sure they did."

"What did you do?" She looked at me like I was crazy.

"What'd I do? I just walked on by. Why pay any attention to ignorant people?" Question asked. Question answered. Beatrice's answer is a perfect example of her innate strength, confidence, and wisdom. She did not ignore out of fear but out of the deep knowledge of her own worth.

Education mattered greatly in the Dilworth family. Beatrice's mother saw that her children had clean clothes and got to school. Beatrice's hard-working, loving mother wanted a better life for her children. B never told me, but the priority of education made sense when I was told that her father couldn't read or write. Searcey Dilworth signed his name with an "X."

B's school was one room with one teacher for all grades. Her brothers and some of the other black children were taken out of school when cotton was in season to pick cotton and help work the land. Black children across the South were provided only discarded books from white schools.

Schools, churches, barber shops, cemeteries, libraries, movie theaters, water fountains, restrooms, ballparks, and phone booths were segregated by Jim Crow laws that appeared in actual legislation that existed, at various times, across the South. Marriage between a white and a black person was outlawed, and books could not be interchanged between white and black schools. In addition, a white nurse had the right to refuse to nurse a Negro patient in a hospital or ward. The Ku Klux Klan was active in Northeast Texas during Beatrice's childhood.

I told B I wished I'd known her parents. Her quick reply was, "I wish you had too." Her parents' determination to raise Christian children with strong values, an education, and pride in who they were played a huge part in Beatrice Dilworth Jones's confidence and strength to confront life. She was a proud product of her parents and family.

When Beatrice and I were talking about her childhood once, she said, "Poor meant not a pot to pee in and not a window to throw it out of." That was the closest she ever came to talking about her family being poor, but this quip was said as fact, not for pity.

Listening to Beatrice talk about her childhood on the small farm in Clarksville made me realize how truly segregated Negroes were from white society. Her parents had no education, nor did they have the chance to improve their lives. They barely made ends meet. However, even during the years of the Depression, when Beatrice was young, there were warm and happy memories of her life on the Dilworth's little farm and in the segregated black community of Haywood. She talked about her immediate family with parents who were strict disciplinarians and held their children to high standards. B's stories always had the backdrop of a close family, a supportive black community, church, and other children with whom she played.

Beatrice grew up in a paradoxical environment: gross injustices on one hand and security and love on the other. I felt deep sadness for Ophelia and Searcey Dilworth, Beatrice's parents. What fears and discouragement might they have felt? Looking at Beatrice's legacy, however, I'm not so sure they did.

5

"I Just Gotta Keep Goin'"

The emphasis on education from Beatrice's parents impacted all eight of their children. Beatrice and her younger sister by two years, O'Deal, were called the "twins." After graduating high school, the twins left Clarksville and went to Amarillo. Beatrice never would tell me that she didn't want to "work the fields anymore," but her daughter told me. Each young girl wanted more education and to have a profession. Their older sister, Madge, lived in Amarillo. Beatrice and her sisters and brothers were the first generation in her family to have a formal education. Ophelia and Searcey surely felt happy and proud of these two daughters as they left to create a new life—one for which their parents never had the opportunity.

Beatrice went to nursing school and became a licensed vocational nurse (LVN), which allowed her to work under doctors and nurses in nursing homes and hospitals and in caregiving in private homes. An LVN education cost less than an RN and took less time to get, so it makes sense that is the route Beatrice chose. O'Deal became a school counselor. How did these two young women pay for school? The answer is easy. They worked.

While in Amarillo, Beatrice began working in a nursing home, and it wasn't long before she met Nathan Jones. She got to know Nathan and began calling him "N.D." The way B said N.D. sounded like "N-dee," one word said fast. They fell in love, married, and moved to Dallas where Nathan had a job contract painting. A new course for the direction of their lives was charted with marriage and this move to Dallas. The new-lyweds moved into a tiny home in Oak Cliff, one of the des-ignated black residential sections of Dallas. Beatrice Dilworth had become Beatrice Jones and soon had her first baby.

Beatrice and Nathan had five children within six years. Five babies, six and under, in their tiny house in Oak Cliff. There were cloth diapers to wash daily, no washing machine or dryer, no dishwasher, and little money. How did Beatrice and Nathan manage? Mothers get exhausted from taking care of one baby. Beatrice had five!

In 1953, '54, '57, '58, and '59, Beatrice gave birth to Curtis, Vera, Don, Marvella, and Rickey. According to Marvella, the home was cramped but always clean, plus the house had a big backyard. The five children all slept in one bedroom, and one small bathroom sufficed for seven people. Nathan worked as a painter while B stayed home caring for the children.

As the children grew, Beatrice and N.D. saw the need to separate the girls and boys. They bought a sofa bed for the boys in the living room. The Jones family of seven lived in this home for over ten years.

One day while visiting my mother, I issued a complaint about my husband to Beatrice. B began to laugh and told me a couple of stories about rough patches in her own marriage. At one point, N.D. would leave after dinner and "go out." Instead of nagging, crying, or allowing resentment to fester, Beatrice took hold of the situation. She had a plan. I was fascinated. "B, what did you do?"

"Well, I got all dressed up fancy. He came home one night and saw me dressed to the nines with a big hat on and everything. N.D. looked at me and said, 'Where are you going?'"

I looked at him and said, "Out. I'm goin' out," as she headed toward the door.

"Where are you going out?"

"I don't know. Just going out. Goodbye." Beatrice left. She did not tell me where she went, but she went out and came home several hours later. N.D. started staying home at night.

Another time, N.D. came home very late. He was crawling in their bedroom window, and B got up and lowered the window down on his hands while saying, "Use the front door." She cracked up every time she told those stories. Only a confident and secure woman could manage five children and a marriage. If B was ever at her wit's end, it did not last long. She thought and acted. Whatever were her methods, N.D. and their five children had great love and respect for this wife and mother.

Supporting a family of seven was a challenge. With five growing children, N.D.'s contract painting did not bring in enough money to feed this hungry family of seven in the 1960s, so Beatrice went out and got a job. Initially she worked at a nursing home and then was hired at Parkland Hospital, working most of the time in the emergency room or labor and delivery.

B told me once about a mother who came in the emergency room holding a baby. The woman held out her baby to Beatrice, "Here. Something's wrong with my baby."

B took the little bundle and looked at the baby. She looked back up at the mother and told her, "Ma'am, your baby is dead." B told that to me factually just as she had to the mother. Because of her training and who she was, she'd remained kind but professional. But B still remembered that day when she held that lifeless baby.

Beatrice would often work two shifts back to back. She'd then have two days off for the children. B did not drive, so she would take two buses to get from home to Parkland and another two buses from Parkland and back home. At some point, B changed from working night shifts at Parkland to cleaning offices at night in an office building nearby. Then she could get home by 11:00 p.m.

Instead of going to bed exhausted when she got home after working two jobs, Beatrice would wake her younger children, one by one, and put them in the bathtub to get them awake. She explained, "I'd sit on the commode and go over their homework with 'em." As she had seen her mother's priority for her eight children to have an education, Beatrice modeled the exact same with her five children. Neither hard work with little pay nor exhaustion kept her from her goal of raising educated children.

One day, a friend of B's asked her why in the world she would agree to be a maid cleaning offices. Her response, a typical Beatrice response was, "I empty shit out of bedpans all day at the hospital. I guess cleaning offices might be a little better." Beatrice did what had to be done and what would be best for her children.

With such a demanding work schedule, how in the world did Beatrice Jones manage children while she was gone? As any commander-in-chief would do, she organized her troops, and everyone had his or her job. The two older children, Curtis and Vera, took care of the younger children after school, see-ing they did their homework before playing. The younger ones knew when the porch light went on, they were to come home.

The years passed, and one day in the early '70s, B insisted she and N.D. go see a doctor because he had not been feeling well for a while. The blow came. N.D. was diagnosed with lung cancer. Life quickly changed in this bustling, busy family. N.D. was soon unable to work, and that left Beatrice the only one bringing home a paycheck. There were five children to feed, bills to pay, and now a sick husband to care for.

Beatrice nursed her sick husband. Marvella explained how this worked, "While Mama was at work, all the kids worked around their classes to fill in and care for him. Mama taught us how to give Daddy his injections and medicine, and we got his meals too. I started taking advanced classes to graduate early. I graduated at sixteen and could then stay home and care for Daddy."

As he got sicker, N.D. wanted a bigger house that would be "better for Mama." They found a three-bedroom home in Pleasant Grove in South Dallas and moved before N.D. died. Beatrice's husband cared the best he could at the end for the wife he loved. Nathan Jones died in 1975.

I asked Marvella if it did not break her mother's heart when he died. "Yes . . . but she had to stay strong for five children. She would go in the garage at times, and I could hear her cry-ing. But she would never let her kids see her cry."

The kids worried about their mama during those sad and difficult days. She would tell them, "Well, I just gotta keep goin'." Beatrice told her kids over and over, "Keep your head up." She worked, put food on the table and kept her children in line. She could discipline with words and looks.

Curtis would drive the younger children to school, and

Beatrice would leave the children's lunch money on a shelf in the hall each morning. Lunch money was labeled "elementary," "junior high," and "high school." She put the children's money in the order of their age. The older and bigger children ate more so needed more money. At times, there wasn't enough money for lunches. Marvella looked back and remembered, "There were no free lunches, but we made it. We became adults by ourselves because Mama was working so hard."

Beatrice began private duty nursing, often caring for elderly parents of doctors. One day in 1979, she went into the bathroom where she was working and fell. She was unresponsive. The man she was caring for called an ambulance. Marvella was teaching at Franklin Junior High when she got the call. She remembers arriving at the hospital and hearing the doctor say, "Your mother is not expected to live, and even if we can save her, she won't be the same."

At some point, B had regained consciousness and looked at the doctor, "I don't want my head shaved." Beatrice Jones had an aneurysm, was going into surgery to save her life, but was still giving orders? The answer is yes.

Marvella remembered the doctor smiling and saying, "We could just shave half your hair then, Mrs. Jones." This doctor had no idea with whom he was dealing. After coming home, "the kids took care of Mama." Not only did Beatrice live, but one day, two months after an aneurysm and emergency surgery, B announced she was ready to go back to work. Miraculously she did.

When B would tell me about her aneurysm, she said all she kept saying over and over was, "Lord, have mercy. Lord, have mercy." For her to tell me about this crisis as many times as she did, let me know how scared she'd been for herself and her five children. N.D. was gone, and she had to take care of her babies.

The prognosis of B's doctor is eerily parallel to what my mother's surgeon told me before my mother's surgery in 2000: "She probably won't make it." Twenty years apart, two indomitable women, one black and one white, both with brain surgeries, shaven heads, and slim chances of recovery. Both women defied medical prognoses and medical odds.

Exactly 20 years after Beatrice's brain surgery, she was called to help care for my mother who'd also had brain surgery. I believe, wholeheartedly, God put Beatrice Jones in my life, my mother's life, and my family's life.

6

Heartbreak

Early in the 1980s, Beatrice brought her elderly parents to Dallas, from their farm in Clarksville, to live with her, so she could care for them. She gave them her bedroom, and she moved into another. Life seemed to be settling into a new routine after the death of N.D. and Beatrice's unbelievable recovery from an aneurysm. She worked private duty nursing during the day and took care of her parents after work. It was a different form of double duty. Beatrice's children pitched in as they had when their father was ill. A year later, Beatrice's mother died and was buried in Clarksville in the black cemetery.

Curtis taught school in the Dallas Independent School District (DISD). One day when he did not feel well, he went to the doctor. At age 29, Curtis, a kind, handsome, and vibrant young man surely was in shock at his diagnosis. Curtis had a brain tumor.

As the oldest of five children, Curtis had done everything

he could to help his mama deal with crisis after crisis. He had been a support and mentor to his brothers and sisters. No one can fathom what this fine young man felt as he trudged home and had to tell his mother his awful news. As Curtis became sicker, he stayed at home where B could take care of her son. Curtis died at home in 1982.

One night two years later, Beatrice got a call from the police. She needed to come downtown and identify her son's body. She told me her other son, Don, had been shot at a gas station. She called her brother, who went to the morgue with her and identified Don's body. Beatrice had lost her husband, barely survived an aneurysm, buried her oldest son, buried both parents, and would now bury another son.

How did Beatrice Jones not give up? How did Beatrice Jones not rage in anger and disbelief? How did Beatrice Jones keep her faith with loss after loss after loss? The blows had kept coming. Beatrice's mother died before Curtis, and her father died between the death of her two beloved sons. Both of her parents had been old and unable to care for themselves. Ophelia and Searcey Dilworth's lives had been honorably lived, and both died in the order expected in life. When Searcey died, he was buried in Clarksville by the side of his wife.

How do I know all this? I finally asked. I had never asked B to tell me about her children and her life until years after I'd known her. When she had talked about her large family, I'd get confused about who was who but became familiar with names and stories. But there were so many, I did not take the time to get them all straight—which were her children, which her grandchildren, which grandchild belonged to which child, and where great-grandchildren fit in the extended family.

I'd made an assumption that hers had been a hard but happy life. That was because of Beatrice's demeanor. I assumed

B was a widow with grown children who were often around with their kids. I did know this huge clan of children, grandchildren, and great-grandchildren gathered at her house on Sundays for dinner after church. Her home was the place family always came.

When I did take the time and energy to ask and listen, I was stunned at what I learned. One morning after Mother was settled and resting in her assisted living facility, B and I began chatting. I asked B about her boys, Curtis, Don, and Rickey, and what they were doing. Her quiet, matter-of-fact reply was, "Curtis and Don are dead." I was stunned, then quiet.

I finally asked what had happened. The way she told me was in B's regular tone of voice as if she were continuing a normal conversation. "Curtis was 29 and a teacher in DISD. He loved his job but got sick, and it was a brain tumor. He died at home. Don was shot at a gas station."

I stuttered, "B, I am so sorry. How in the world did you ever survive?" How did this woman who delighted in caring for erratic elderly people, day after day with great patience and kindness, deal with her own tragedy?

I will never forget her answer. I can still picture Beatrice as we talked, and she answered my question. I can still picture our chairs angled toward each other with the sun coming in the window behind me. I was focused on B, truly anxious to know how a mother survived the loss of two sons.

"B, how did you go on with your life?"

"When Curtis died, they came and asked me if I wanted to see the hearse take him away. I told them 'What do you think? I've just seen my son die in my house, and now I'd want to see them take him away? No.' After his funeral service, I was sitting in my rocking chair at home, and someone asked me what I was going to do tomorrow. 'I'm going to work.' I was told that was crazy, I couldn't go to work. I told 'em, 'Well, what'd you want me to do? Stay home and sit in this rockin' chair all day and feel sorry for myself? I'll be at work.' I had to get over it; they weren't coming back. I'd said, 'God, if you're not goin' to intervene, please go ahead and take 'em.'"

I was still quiet and simply looked at this woman I thought I knew, the woman who came to work every day with energy and a smile. Beatrice had many sad, dark days. She is tough, but she loved deeply and treasured her family. And she "kept movin' forward."

That conversation helped me see that people who come into my life have layers upon layers of living within them, that I have no idea of the hurts and pain they have endured or the joys that have made their hearts soar. Beatrice Jones was a survivor. Life never kept her down. What I saw, though, is that Beatrice Jones did not only survive but continued to live.

Beatrice was a Christian with an unshakable faith. To her, it was simple: "If I didn't love Him, I wouldn't serve Him. God loves His children and has a time and plan for their lives. When life is hard, God walks with His children." That was her strength, always. That was why B had refused ever to feel sorry for herself. Did she grieve and feel sad? Without question, but Beatrice Jones "kept going" and "kept her head up" no matter what. Most of all, she trusted God with her life and her children's lives.

Beatrice loved and was devoted to her church, Salem Baptist. She had always had a church family who surrounded her with love and support. She'd gone to Sunday School and church every Sunday, taught Sunday School, served meals, and been there Wednesday nights for Bible Study. B would often talk about Reverend Campbell and what he had said or done.

On a lighter note, B still had firm convictions about death. "That's one appointment you won't be late for," she announced to me one day after someone had been late arriving.

Another time, she told me the story of telling her mischievous grandson he'd better start behaving. Right away, the little boy asked, "Grandmama, will my name still be in God's book since I was bad?"

B's quick response was, "Yep, God 'll say 'I've got your name right here, and the rain won't wash it away.'" This little boy had no more concerns about where he would spend eternal life.

B loved her little dog, Cinnamon. She would laugh and tell stories about Cinnamon to Mom and me. One Monday when I came by, B seemed quiet. I asked if she was all right, and she told me Cinnamon had been run over that weekend. I was sad for B. She was sad, too, but said, "Well, I don't want to get run over like Cinnamon. So she had to go on. I'm okay. We didn't come in the world together, and we're not gonna leave together. God has a plan. She's gone, so my job is to look forward."

7

The Blue Chair

As I absorbed more and more of Beatrice the person and not just Beatrice the caregiver, I saw what a narrow world I'd lived in my whole life. My grandparents had lived in Northeast Texas, and in the 1950s and '60s, I'd seen the black section of their town and small surrounding farms when we took evening drives to see the cattle on my grandfather's farm. Clarksville was close to Cooper, and its black section and small surrounding farms would have been much the same as the black farms I'd seen outside of Cooper. I realized this strong woman who had lived in poverty, endured social injustice, and survived great heartache had a life so very different from mine. I was humbled.

This was the woman who'd sat by my mother's hospital bed for weeks and weeks. After a months-long, arduous, but miraculous recovery, Mother was released from skilled nursing, with limitations, to move to an assisted living facility. I asked Beatrice if she could keep helping Mom once she left the hospital. Although able to walk slowly on her walker by herself, Mother's short-term memory had been affected, and she would stand and unintentionally forget to use her walker. She was weak and frail, and since I could not take the chance of her falling again, Beatrice consented to stay with Mother during the day as she adjusted to new living accommodations. To have Beatrice with her gave me huge relief and the ability to return to a somewhat normal life.

On B's off weeks, Patrice or B's daughter, Vera, filled in. The assisted living facility was small and clean, and there was a window in Mom's small bedroom that looked out onto a garden. Moving day came, and Beatrice drove Mother to her new home while I directed movers.

At times, I would stop to check on Mom in the morning before B came. Mother would be sitting at a table by herself, eating the same breakfast every day, raisin bran with banana, cranberry juice, and coffee. These were special times together with her. B arrived right at 9:00 with no more complaints from Mom about being late, and she would often join us in the dining room as Mom finished her breakfast.

As a matter of fact, my mother did not want Beatrice there at all, and her stubborn streak emerged. I'm sure she ruminated for several days about her decision to let B go. That was Mother's way. The morning of B's firing, Mom was sitting up in her bed reading the newspaper, and B was sitting quietly in a chair beside the bed. My mother put the paper down, looked right at B, and instructed, "You can go now. I don't need you anymore."

"Mrs. Tompkins, I can't leave you."

"Yes, you can. I told you, you could. You can go home now."

"No, I can't. You didn't hire me. Mary hired me."

"Hmmph, Mary. Well, then she's paying you with my

money!" Mother had no choice but to look back at her newspaper. That was the end of that conversation.

Beatrice stayed, but that didn't mean Mom liked it nor did she have to pay any attention to B. She allowed B to help her when needed but was not happy about it. B was so tickled one afternoon as she described their walks to meals or activities. "I help your mother get on the walker. Once we're in the hall, she won't walk with me. She walks in the middle of the hall, and when she turns the corner, she lifts that walker, jerks it around, and glares back at me." I could picture this. My mother had never yelled or argued loudly, but we sure knew when she was mad. I loved my mother being back to the mother I'd always known, and I loved B for letting my mother be my mother and being fine with that. Her job was to help and be a companion, and that's just what she did.

The assisted living facility had a beautiful grand piano in the large dining area. Mother was a gifted pianist who could play almost anything by ear. Playing the piano was her gift, but it was her hobby, too, and what she'd always done when exhausted from teaching, cooking, and parenting. Our home was filled with music every day ranging from hymns to holiday and patriotic music to children's songs to "Twelfth Street Rag."

Several months before, after Mother had been transferred to the Jackson Building, my brother suggested he place Mom's wheelchair at the piano. This was soon after her surgery, and I was dubious about the idea. I wanted B to interfere, but she calmly watched. It was Christmas Day, and my mother hadn't even known what to do with gifts we'd placed on the table for her. She had just looked at them, confused, having no idea to remove the wrapping paper and receive a gift. I feared even more confusion if she were placed at the piano, but my brother wanted to try.

In front of the piano, Mother frowned quizzically at the keyboard. Her brain was trying valiantly to process what was in front of her. Sitting by her, I raised my hand and played slowly, with one finger, the melody of "Jingle Bells." I looked at her. She slowly lifted her hands and placed her unsure fingers on the keys. Again, I plunked out the same few notes. Mother, tentatively, put fingers of both hands on the notes; sluggish neurons were fighting to awaken.

She began, ever so slowly, to play a version of "Jingle Bells" no one had ever heard. Yes, it was all the wrong notes but correct timing and fingering. She knew! Her brain was working hard, and she had connected with her love of the piano! After she played her rendition of "Jingle Bells," Mother instinctively knew that something was wrong and remained confused. She turned, looked at me, and said slowly, "Mary, I need to practice." I smiled because my mother had said to me, ten million times, when I took piano lessons and played that I needed to practice. B just watched, taking it all in.

There had been recognition! The Christmas gift to Danny, my brother, and all of us had been the scene we just witnessed—a Christmas miracle on the seventh floor of the Jackson Building. Mother had figured out that the notes produced music. She tried again with the same result, looked at me, and I can still see those gentle brown eyes as she said clearly, "Music is in here" and placed her hand on her heart. Danny was giddy with excitement and encouragement, B was smiling big, and I was quiet. That was one of the most touching moments of Mother's entire recovery, and it gave watchful nurses an option to occupy her rather than using restraints in bed. Beatrice had watched all of this and now understood another aspect of my unique mother.

Once she moved to assisted living, Mother began to play

again, this time with correct timing and notes. Seeing her once again at the piano was wonderful. Music did feed her soul as well as delighting the residents and staff when she played in the dining room. B told me one day that they'd ask Mom to play at a sing-along, and she'd agreed. The large activities' calendar would say, "Sunday Night Sing-Along with Mary Tompkins at the Piano." Unbelievable from where she'd been one year before.

At the sing-along, Mother would play, rarely looking at the keyboard. My job had been to make song books from my mother's music that included patriotic, military, and '30s and '40s songs such as "Five Foot Two, Eyes of Blue." I'd stand by Mom and get the residents involved in selecting a song and singing. Mom and I were a good team and had fun. The next morning, B would always want to know how the "sing-song" went and chuckle as she pictured the two of us leading the sing-along.

Beatrice knew she could always take Mom to the piano and occupy her. Mother loved to play hymns and sacred music and was at the piano in the dining area playing an old-time favorite, "The Old Rugged Cross," one Sunday morning before lunch. An elderly man walked up and started dancing. B said his dancing distressed my mother. Of course, she would have thought his happy dancing disrespectful to the music of this reverent hymn. The picture of Mom playing "The Old Rugged Cross" and frowning as this strange man danced joyfully to the sacred hymn makes me laugh even today.

I am so thankful Beatrice was there with Mom because B is the one who would tell me delightful and funny stories of things that happened during Mother's days. People assume assisted living facilities are sad and boring places. They're not. Yes, the residents are elderly and slower. Some can't hear or see well, but there is life. I learned that from B's watchful eye.

One of B's stories involved a church service that was scheduled every Sunday afternoon. B and Mom always attended, along with 10 to 15 other residents. One Sunday, B said she almost fell off her chair because of one of the funniest situations she'd ever seen. While the minister was preaching, a lady who was hard of hearing said something a couple of times in a loud voice to her neighbor. The third interruption from this woman was too much for another lady who was sitting on the other side of B and trying to listen to the minister. "What'd he say?" said the hard-of-hearing woman to her neighbor.

The irritated but feisty, 90-year-old woman leaned over B, glared at the offender, and said to her in an even louder voice, "Shut up!" The minister's eyes got big, all was quiet for a moment, and he then continued preaching as if nothing had happened. As B told me this story, she'd have to pause because she'd get so tickled recalling it. I loved that I could get stories of my mother's days, knowing there was interesting life in the residence where she lived.

Beatrice told me these stories because she observed daily life and people. She didn't rush, nor did she rush others. B didn't mind waiting, and she wasn't bored caring for elderly people. She had a compassion and love for her fellow man and saw people's interactions as real life.

A managerial change where Mother was living caused another move. The new assisted living where we moved Mom was larger with a bedroom and a living area. This was where I had the conversation with B learning about the deaths of her two sons, Curtis and Don. This was where I learned my mother wanted to be buried in Dallas, not Corpus Christi where my dad was buried. That was the room where the famous blue chair arrived.

Soon after Mother's and B's latest move, I went to Colorado with my husband as wonderful relief from hot Dallas summers. At the end of this particular summer, he returned to work, and I decided to stay in Crested Butte to hike, see the aspens turn, and return home at the end of September. I'd never been in the mountains in autumn.

To pass the time, I signed up for a course at Western State, a small college in Gunnison, 28 miles south of Crested Butte. With four kids either married, working, or in college, and a husband who stayed on the golf course, I felt a new freedom. I was living in a small town deep in the Rocky Mountains doing my thing for once. The drive back and forth to Gunnison in the quiet, early mornings three times a week was a spiritual and stunningly beautiful experience. I never tired of the magnificent setting no matter the weather—a rising sun over the mountains, low clouds, rain, or snow. I loved it all—and was excited about my short but new adventure. I kept up with Mother and B by phone each day.

One day after my class in Gunnison, I stopped at Walmart. Crested Butte didn't have a stop light, much less a pharmacy, so Walmart in Gunnison was where I got most everything I needed. As I was walking toward the paper goods, all of a sudden, I saw an area of medical supplies that I hadn't noticed before. As part of the inventory, they had a chair that was a recliner. It wasn't big and bulky, nor was it naugahyde. It was the perfect size for my mother and was covered in a soft, blue velvety type of fabric. The chair had pockets on the side where a book, glasses, or miscellaneous items could be kept, and it had a remote for adjusting.

Mother's living area had her upright sofa and two straight dining room chairs. What a perfect addition this chair would be for her! Plus it was blue, her favorite color. This discovery was serendipitous. The chair was shipped the following day to The Plaza, Mom's new residence. I knew she'd love it.

Several days later, my phone rang. B was laughing so hard she could hardly talk. "B, what's going on?" I had not told them about the surprise I'd ordered. B relayed one of the all-time best stories of their time together.

Two men had knocked on the door with the large parcel for Mrs. Dan Tompkins, my mother. Mother told them, in her schoolteacher voice, she had not ordered anything, that it was a mistake, and to take it back. B looked at the label and told her it was from me. Mom was mad and reiterated she didn't want this delivery and to take it back now!

"Mary's just spent more of my money. I don't want that big thing, whatever it is." The men had unpacked the chair and didn't know what to do. Even when she saw the chair, Mother said, "I don't want it. Take it away." She was adamant. Beatrice was befuddled but only momentarily.

"Mrs. Tompkins, Mary has sent this to you because she thought you'd like it. You can't send it back."

"Yes, I can."

"Well, I'm not going to do that. Mary went to the trouble to send this to you. It's unpacked, and they are going to put it in here, right over there by the window. Look how pretty it is, and it's a gift to you from Mary." My mother sat displeased with pursed lips and arms crossed on her upright sofa. The men and packaging left, and B and Mother were alone in the room with the unwelcome blue chair.

"Well! I'm not going to sit in it!" There was only a pause before the Beatrice I'd come to know took over.

"That's all right. If you're not going to sit in it, I think I will." B went over, sat down, and leaned back against the soft, blue of the recliner. After a few minutes, B began her soliloquy, "Oh, this chair is so nice. Ohhhh, it's so comfortable." B located the remote that allowed the blue chair to recline. "Look at me, Mrs. Tompkins. I'm glad you don't like it. I think I'll just stay . . . here . . . all . . . day. This is the most comfortable chair I've ever sat in. I can sit up and then lie back. I think I'll just close my eyes for a few minutes and take . . . a . . . little nap."

Although my mom never turned her head to B, her slitted eyes shifted over, and she saw Beatrice's pleasure in the unwanted blue chair. I don't know whether it was ten minutes or thirty minutes or what else B might have said or not said. What I do know is that it wasn't that long before my mother, still displeased, spoke, "Oh well . . . all right. I guess I'll sit in that thing for a minute since it's here, and Mary sent it."

"Are you sure? I'm really likin' this chair."

"Yes, I am sure. I'll try it out just for a few minutes." From that day, in the fall of 2003 to 2009, my mother sat in that blue chair every day and mostly all day until the day before she died.

After breakfast, Mom began reading the paper in her new blue chair, reclining with her feet propped up, looking like royalty while B was content to just be there or look at a magazine. They would talk if Mother wanted to. Beatrice had this unique gift of kindness and timing with every patient for whom she ever cared.

Mother liked quiet but liked to visit when I'd come by. She'd be in her new blue chair, eager to hear news about me and her grandchildren. One morning, I'd stopped to visit, and the three of us—Mom, B, and I—got into a fun conversation talking about who-knows-what. My mother had been an excellent student and the daughter who followed rules at home and school. She practiced her piano and did her homework.

Because she was who she was, I thought it was time to shake

things up, and I shifted the conversation to asking a different type of question about my mom's life. Where I thought of the question I don't know, but it ramped up the conversation into one of the most hilarious the three of us ever had. I asked my mother if she had ever smoked a cigarette, something I was sure she never had done, but the conversation needed some spark. I can still hear Mom as she quietly answered and told me a story I love to this day. She always spoke slowly and thoughtfully.

"Yes, Mary, I did." With my mouth wide open, she continued, "When I took the train to Kerrville from Cooper for my first teaching job, I had to spend the night in Kerrville before catching the bus the next day for Junction. I decided I would just go buy some cigarettes and see what all my friends liked about them. So I did. I smoked my first cigarette, and it was my last. I burned my eyebrows!" I couldn't believe what I'd just heard. Beatrice, Mother, and I were doubled over laughing, and I saw a part of my mother she'd not ever allowed me to see before.

Now Beatrice had a story to tell about cigarettes. She, too, had gotten hold of some cigarettes when she was young and experimenting with her first one. She was outside the family farmhouse in Clarksville, supposedly, hanging sheets out to dry, but her purpose was more nefarious than that. B was safely hidden by the sheets, had lit her cigarette, and was happily smoking away. Her mother called and came out to get her. Beatrice could laugh and talk at the same time, which was hilarious in itself, and the way she told her story was as if it happened yesterday.

"Oh good Lord. I didn't know what to do. I was so surprised Mama was coming out that I threw that cigarette up in the air to get rid of it, and it went down my back! I burned my back." She couldn't quit laughing as she remembered this story, and her wonderful, infectious laugh only added to the comedy of stories we were all delighting in. Burned eyebrows and a burned back. These stories from B and my mother sharing a part of their lives created a warmth and closeness with the three of us that morning.

I wanted to participate too. I told my story of smoking or trying to smoke my first cigarette. I was in the backseat of a car with a bunch of girls. I was sitting in the middle, and we were all talking, smoking, and singing along with the radio. One of the girls said she smelled something burning. We all started looking around, and my good friend, Cyd, turned to me and said, "Oh good grief, Mary, you lit the wrong end of the cigarette, and you're smoking it backwards!" I was not so cool after all.

Mother, B, and I each had stories, but Mother's and B's were classics. This particular morning held one of those rare golden moments of love, sharing, and joy that can never be planned or duplicated. They just happen. This wonderful conversation occurred on a routine day. What a precious memory that morning of laughter is.

8

Safety Pins, Pursed Lips, and Chocolate

"**B**eatrice, could you use any of Mom's furniture that won't go with her if she survives? Whatever is going to happen, it's certain she won't be living alone, so it's time to close down her apartment at the independent living facility."

"I can use everything you'll give me. Sure I can." I was not used to such directness, and I liked it.

Giving Mom's furniture to B felt so right. With Mother still in the hospital, we still had no idea of the length of recovery or even if she would recover. We did know her days of independent living were over. B's faithfulness, goodness, and support through my back surgery and now Mom's uncertain recovery were invaluable. Words could never express the gratitude we all felt for the dedication to my mother and the relief to me.

With a loved one's life hanging in the balance, nice furniture and draperies don't matter—they're just things. They're not the person you love, the eyes that look at you and love you back.

The few pieces of furniture that had meaning to Mother and would stay with her, assuming she made it, would be stored. We would fit her piano in wherever she lived because music was part of who she was. Even if she couldn't play, she might look at her piano and feel the music she loved, whatever cognition returned.

I tackled the stack of papers that was overwhelming. Twenty-year-old bank statements had been saved in grocery sacks so old, the thick paper had become soft. Mother's birth certificate and bills were mixed in with multiple letters from solicitors and personal mail. Before I went over the edge, I called my dear cousin for reinforcement. Linda tackled the paper and mail, and I tackled Mom's closets and personal items.

Looking into Mom's two closets, I sucked in a big breath and slammed the doors. Not only had she saved every piece of mail but also every piece of clothing she'd had for decades— even the bathing suit she'd worn in the '50s which she said she couldn't wear anymore "because it had a hole in the knee." Overwhelmed again. I needed even more help and asked Beatrice if she could come one afternoon after leaving the hospital. I needed additional moral support before my emotions interfered with my task. B was not only moral support, but she also helped balance a dreaded task with laughter. Perspective is a lifesaver.

My mother had been a beautiful seamstress. She'd made clothes and spent hours altering or remaking clothes that didn't fit to save money. She'd made dresses for me when I was little. She made my first doll, Nancy, and made clothes for my other dolls. At home, Mother was either in the kitchen, at the piano, or at her sewing machine. She kept what she bought—all of it! Although her vision prevented her sewing in her 80s, she had kept ripping and ripping out seams of so many clothes that needed altering, holding the seams together with safety pins and thinking or hoping, someday she might remake them. These clothes were all jammed in two closets so tightly, I couldn't even move the hangars.

I warned B before I opened "Closet One." She said, "Let's get going." When she saw the shiny gleam of the million safety pins holding ripped seams together in pantsuit after pantsuit, dress after dress, Beatrice burst into peals of laughter. I, too, began to laugh. Soon we were both laughing so hard over the millions of safety pins, I had to wipe happy tears away.

"B, I don't think these clothes will fit you, but would you like to have them?"

"I'll take whatever you'll give me. If I don't use 'em, somebody can."

Beatrice Jones was an independent and proud woman who never asked for anything. Ever. But if you offered, you'd better mean it. She'd take it and find a use for it.

Clearing out the majority of my mother's clothes, clothes that had touched her skin, carried an emotional pull that going through papers did not. Even the clothes she'd recently worn, I never knew if she'd wear again. Her prognosis was still up in the air.

Miraculously Mother slowly did recover and regain her memory, against all odds. Yet for nine years, wherever she lived, she would occasionally look in her well maintained and organized closet, then look dejectedly at B and me, shake her head in disgust, and say, "I can't believe someone stole all my clothes. I still miss my red velour jogging suit." Jogging suit? As she'd shake her head one more time, Beatrice and I would exchange furtive glances and change the subject.

Beatrice Jones put those stacks and stacks and more stacks of clothing in the mission closet of Salem Baptist Church. I believe Beatrice's donation, and Mom's unknown donation, gave missionaries needed clothing they were able to repair. First, however, they had to remove a million shiny safety pins.

Beatrice Jones was 70 years old when she came to the hospital that first afternoon when Mom was in ICU and the afternoon she helped me clean out Mother's closet. She was nearing 80 when Mother died. B worked full-time caregiving in the eighth decade of her life.

Several years later, long after the safety pin story and after Mom had recovered enough to be in assisted living, she got to the point where she needed full-time care. Her health was declining, so we moved Mom to an apartment close to my home. B's other elderly patient had died, so now she was able to work every weekday. Patrice took nights during the week, Vera took Saturdays and Sundays, and Marvella came on Saturday and Sunday nights. Three generations of Beatrice's family were caring for my mother—Beatrice; her two daughters, Vera and Marvella; and one granddaughter, Patrice. Three generations of a family entered my mom's small apartment every week to care for her. This family was a true gift to my mother as well as my brother in California and me.

There were stories that were constantly told by each of the caregivers, but no one had as much time and as many stories with Mother as Beatrice. And no one could tell a story like Beatrice. She told me stories that would make us both laugh together, and I can still hear Beatrice's lively, engaging laugh. One story that became funnier and funnier over the years is the story of the red convertible. It all began with my having car trouble.

Car trouble is never fun and especially when the problem cannot be repaired quickly. My car was in the car hospital. That morning, my husband, accidentally, took his car keys when he left town, so there was no car for Mary. How was I to lead my all-important life? Quite a conundrum.

Yellow Cab dropped me at the Hertz counter near Love Field. As I put the key in my rented, boring, gray economy car, my eyes lit on a reflection of bright red in front of me. The bright red belonged to a shiny Mustang convertible.

Back to the counter, I marched. I slapped those economy keys down on the counter and in no time at all, I clasped a new key to my breast—the key to that shiny, red, Mustang convertible. It took a mere thirty seconds for this bright red Mustang convertible to change my personality. Driving off in my new acquisition, I had a new-found confidence. I was ready for adventure.

First came a brilliant idea that involved Beatrice and my 94-year-old mother. My mother sat day after day in her blue chair, except when B and I, or just B, took her to the doctor or the hairdresser. The only change in Mother's routine was the rotation of caregivers. I let Beatrice know ahead of time about my genius idea—a trip in the shiny, red, Mustang convertible to Sonic for a hamburger and limeade. B grinned, taking any suggestion I made in stride.

My mother was not an adventurous woman. She was calm, genteel, and cautious. In the past, when I had suggested an adventure, she would be doubtful but go along, and we always ended up having a good time. I knew today would be another successful outing. I was wrong.

The beautiful, spring day was perfect as I came to get B and Mom. I told Mother the plan. Yes, doubtful, but B got Mom on her walker and down to the garage while I got the car and parked by the elevator door. As B helped Mother into the car, I turned to share her smile. There was no smile. No smile? We're in a shiny, red Mustang convertible! How can there be no smile?

There was a knowing smile on Beatrice's face.

B buckled Mom in the front seat and adjusted herself in the back. Ready for adventure, I knew Mother's delight would emerge. No smile. At a stop light three minutes later, I turned to now share her smile. Still no smile. Instead of the anticipated delight, Mom was looking straight ahead, lips pursed. I knew that look well. Not a good sign. I looked back at B. My genius plan for an outing was going awry.

I was confused. Beatrice was not. She understood every nuance of my mother. When I looked back at B, I realized the problem as she whispered, "It's her hair." I noticed Mom's hands over her ears protecting those few little silver hairs sprayed in place in her newly coiffed hair and then remembered those net wind bonnets she'd always worn to keep her weekly do in place. But there was hardly any wind.

Remembering Winston Churchill's resolve, "Never, never, never, never . . . give up. . . ." I realized I must not give up on my mission either. Mom would come around and enjoy our adventure in the shiny, red, Mustang convertible. I just knew it.

To jumpstart excitement for our road trip of a mere two miles, I saw a bed of beautiful, multicolored petunias and pulled in the driveway of the Dallas Woman's Club. I cajoled, "Mom, look at those beautiful flowers."

"I see them." Lips still pursed. Beatrice held her composure but barely. Her shoulders were shaking. She was enjoying every minute of my mom's martyred tolerance and my discomfort.

I persevered. I would take a picture of B and Mom in the

shiny, red Mustang convertible on this beautiful day. Then she would *have* to smile. Wrong again. No smile. I asked Mom to wave for the picture, and she raised her arm at a 90-degree angle like a soldier obeying a command. Compliant noncompliance. I took the damn picture. Beatrice and the petunias were the only ones smiling.

My stubborn streak emerged. I was on a mission for fun, and fun we would have. As we headed to Sonic, the shiny, red Mustang convertible crept along at a snail's pace to protect the few strands of an elderly woman's hair. How can a mother and daughter be so different? I loved my hair blowing in the springtime breeze while riding in this sporty, red car that would give anyone pleasure—almost anyone.

At Sonic, we pulled in an open slot. I was nearing mental exhaustion but asked hopefully, "Mom, what about a burger and limeade?" I was back to cajoling.

"Yes, I would like that." Martyred and still with pursed lips. My intentions had been pious, but my intentions now were just to abort. Winston, this mission has proved impossible.

Did Mom see riding in a convertible as unladylike? As immoral? Or was it just her hair? Who knows? B had suspected this could happen as we drove out of the garage. She knew her patient but kept quiet, never interfering with me or my plans. If only Mother had that tacky piece of purple net, her beloved "wind bonnet" to protect her hair, maybe this short adventure would have been successful. Just maybe.

Beatrice Jones laughed uproariously at our red Mustang convertible adventure ever since it occurred, 15 years ago. As she settled into her 80s, B began having memory problems herself. For her 86th birthday, I gave her two framed pictures I'd taken on that fateful day when B, Mom, and I had stopped to see the spring flowers and have an adventure in the shiny red Mustang convertible. I didn't know if she'd remember, but when B unwrapped her gift and saw the pictures of Mom, herself, and the flowers in the red convertible . . . once again, I heard her full, wonderful laugh. She remembered.

Another story that kept Beatrice, Marvella, Vera, my kids, and me in stitches began one slow afternoon. Visitors were rare for Mom and B, and the knock on the door was a welcome sound. Beatrice smiled as Sally, my daughter, walked in with a thoughtful gift for her grandmother. She handed Mama T a small round box covered in tan fabric with red, white, and blue beads forming an American flag on top. The broad smile on my patriotic mother's face showed surprise and pleasure at her gift, yet there was more to come. When Mama T took the top off the box, she found it filled with Hershey kisses. Her broad smile changed to a beaming smile. Beatrice smiled too. She, as well as Sally, knew my mother's nonsecret love—chocolate.

Beatrice had watched Mom eat chocolate ice cream for dessert every day after lunch and dinner. That's how she knew the Hershey kisses would be a hit, but none of us knew how big a hit. Sally's round box with the American flag on top became a treasure of her grandmother's. But every time B looked at the box on the shelf, she shook her head at what the box brought into her patient's life—chocolate candy.

The original Hershey kisses from Sally were gone in two days. Beatrice got a kick out of Mom's pleasure from her gift. When I asked B what happened to the candy, she said, in a tone of exasperation that indicated I should have known, "She ate 'em! What'd you think happened?"

The Hershey kisses had become lunch and dinner. For a couple of days, this didn't matter, but when Mom wasn't eating at mealtime, I found myself encouraging her to eat her vegetables just as she had done to me as a child. To avoid discussion, she'd agree, "I will, Mary." Immobility cannot stop a determined and conniving elderly woman. Beatrice watched the plan unfold that my mother hatched from her blue chair.

Beatrice and I refused to get more chocolate for Mom, so she simply worked around us. B stopped Mom's requests for chocolate, cold. She said, "I don't have the money to get you chocolate candy because you don't pay me enough." No response from Mother because no one was getting more of her money.

Vera, Marvella, and Patrice were younger, kind women who were vulnerable to pleasing my mother. Mom would sweetly ask, "Would one of you please bring me some chocolate candy when you come next? But don't tell Beatrice or Mary." They didn't want to disappoint a rare request from a sweet elderly woman, so every weekend one of them would walk in with a week's supply of chocolate, which Mother would surreptitiously slip in the outside pocket of her blue recliner. Usually, it was a Hershey bar with pieces easy to break apart.

The tell-tale signs began to appear to B and me—chocolate around Mom's mouth, in her teeth, and under her fingernails. Mother would slip her left hand slowly down the side of the recliner to pull out a piece of the giant Hershey bar that had been supplied. I noticed her sneaky move one day and looked at B. She just shrugged as if fighting the chocolate battle was a lost cause. I shrugged, too, because my mom thought all was normal, having no idea we were onto her and that evidence was all over her face and hands.

For fun and diversion, I'd ask, "Mom, have you had any chocolate today?"

"No, Mary, I haven't. Have you?" Not only did this honest woman turn to outright lying, she smoothly switched the topic to me. Dementia? Not when it concerned chocolate. I'd shake my head, just like B, and go get a wet washcloth to clean Mom's mouth. Then I'd change the subject because I knew by her countenance this topic was hers to win. B took care of the chocolate under her fingernails. Mom even regressed to war days of rationing and was able to portion her giant Hershey bar so it would last until the next week's contraband arrived.

I discovered the first source of Mom's stash one Saturday morning when I'd stopped by to write checks to B and the crew. I was sitting by Mother chatting when Vera arrived and called out from the front door, "Mrs. Tompkins, I brought you your chocolate candy." Ah-ha! It was Vera!

"Mary, she asked me to. I couldn't say no." I shook my head. There was an undercover chocolate cartel operating under my nose, headed by an elderly woman who happened to be my mother and Beatrice's patient. Cartel suppliers were caregivers. B and I let it alone and watched the secretive cartel continue operating. Marvella and Vera were both suppliers and Patrice less so since she worked nights during the week.

I still bought the Blue Bell chocolate ice cream, and B continued to serve Mom her dessert after every lunch and dinner. B would chuckle from the kitchen telling me, "Every day I hear her say as she eats the same dessert, 'Oh this is *so* good.' Same chocolate ice cream every day, twice a day, and says the same thing every time. I know it's comin', just wait till she says it. Your mother is funny about her ice cream." Chocolate and my mom.

I told each of my kids about their grandmother's undercover life, and they loved it. Their grandmother had followed the straight and narrow all her life, and now she had no compunction about lying, even when chocolate was clearly visible. Mom protected her turf, thinking she was safe—and she was.

My kids adopted my game. "Mama T, have you had any chocolate today?"

Looking right at them, "No, I haven't." They'd get tickled at their grandmother, but this topic was a great conversation starter. They'd talk to their grandmother while Beatrice got a washcloth and cleaned their grandmother's hands and mouth.

9

The Pink Purse

Mothers never change. It doesn't matter the age. Mothers worry. My mother's apartment was near my home, which made it easy to check on her frequently. She'd taken care of me her whole life. Now it was my turn.

The funny thing is that when I came by to check on things, even when I hadn't felt like going, I always left feeling better. Beatrice would look at me and start laughing her happy laugh as I entered. That never failed to put a smile on my face. The security I felt when B was there is indescribable. I knew my mother was being taken care of. Beatrice Jones's care, compassion, and faithfulness gave my mother love and security.

B would be doing wash, watching a preacher on television, fixing a meal, helping my mother, or quietly reading her Bible. Beatrice knew my mother liked quiet. Mom did not like a lot of chatter unless from me or my children, so much of the time, B left Mom alone reading the newspaper or *Anne of Green Gables,* a favorite book since childhood. Or Mom might be dozing in her blue recliner.

When my mom read or dozed, this gave Beatrice time. I'd often see her Bible open on a side table. Beatrice didn't talk about that or ever push her Christianity on anyone. She simply lived her faith. But if you asked her how she dealt with certain aspects of her life, she would clearly tell you.

B knew when my mother needed company, and then they would talk. If Mom was worried about something, like my driving by myself to Colorado, B listened and gave wise counsel that comforted my mother. Beatrice was not only her caregiver but also her friend.

Lizzie, my red English Cocker, would at times accompany me on late afternoon visits. Beatrice always smiled when I walked in with Lizzie because she knew Mom was not a dog person but tolerated Lizzie since I was there. My dog was small and would sit obediently as Mom and I visited. B would occasionally come in, and the three of us would visit and giggle like three best friends.

One particular cold winter afternoon, the sun was going down, and the three of us were having a pleasant chat in Mom's cozy room. There was a pause, and B began to smile as my mother turned, looked at me, and morphed into the worry mother. She calmly mandated, "Mary, it's getting dark. You need to go home." What did she just say? I was confused while B was trying her best not to burst out laughing. I turned into a defensive adolescent.

"Mother. I am 60 years old. I can take care of myself. I am just fine and don't need to go home just because it's dark."

"Mary, you need to go home now. It'll be dark soon." Her eyes remained steady on me as she stuck to her command. Beatrice delighted in this short exchange. She knew my mother well—the elderly mother who still worried about her children who, by the way, were 60 and 66. Ninety-five years old and my mother still wanted me home by dark. Good grief. Mother's brow was furrowed with worry and Beatrice's brow lifted in glee. I half-smiled, rolled my eyes, and kissed my mother goodbye. Lizzie and I walked home. We were home by dark.

The next afternoon as I walked in, I realized something was going on. "B, what is so funny?"

"Remember yesterday when your mother told you to go on home 'cuz it was gettin' dark?"

"Yes."

"After you'd gone, I asked your mother, 'Mrs. Tompkins, it is getting dark. Don't you want me to go on home too? You know, before it gets dark.'"

"No, B, I don't."

"You told Mary you didn't want her out after dark. I thought you wouldn't want me out after dark either." Mother's answer was immediate and succinct.

"You're not Mary." For once, my mother's statement ended a conversation with B. Beatrice knew exactly what she was doing. She had loved that simple, short dialog between Mom and me and couldn't wait to continue it herself. She also couldn't wait to tell me. That's why B was chortling with delight the next day when I came in.

Beatrice had a unique sense of humor that allowed her to delight in conversations with her elderly patients. She had a lively but gentle way of teasing the patients for whom she cared. She allowed the elderly to respond and be who they were. No judgment. She treated elderly people as if they were her peers, not like old people who couldn't think or reason.

At age 95, my mother's calm, direct, and loving response to Beatrice is a treasured memory. I am thankful to Beatrice Jones for telling me this story. I can still see the late afternoon sun going down, the room where I sat visiting with Mom, Lizzie on the floor, and Mom's quiet directive to me. I can also visualize B's subsequent conversation with my mother. I smile. I miss those mundane but memorable days with B and my mother.

"Mary, it's getting dark" is a simple and funny story, but it has the deeper impact of highlighting three personalities, ending with Beatrice having so much fun with Mom. It's also a story of a mother's love for her daughter.

I loved that Beatrice could tease with my mother and loved that Beatrice would tell me these stories. Life was not dull in apartment #142 with an elderly woman and her caregiver, as most would expect. I felt secure knowing Beatrice and my mother had a trusting and warm relationship.

As I look back, there are so many memories with my unassuming mother and B. Mom and Beatrice were opposite personalities—one quiet and thoughtful, one who could be quiet or talk forever and had a one-sentence answer for any question or problem, social, political, or religious issue.

Occasionally while in her 90s, Mom's interest in clothes, fabric, and fashion would emerge, and B would drive her to Draper's & Damon's to shop. Mom added a lovely purple and bright pink wool suit to her wardrobe, neither of which required silver safety pins. One of these suits, she was buried in. When B would report on their day, she would tell me they'd gone shopping and then shake her head and say, "You know where we went. That same place she loves—'Draper and Diamond.'" I chuckled to myself every time I heard B say her name for the store.

Speaking of Mom's interest in clothes and fashion reminded me of one of the best stories of B, Mom, Vera, and me. This story began when Mother got a new purse but has its seeds in my childhood.

Patent leather shoes were an understood fact of life when I was little. Patent leather Sunday School shoes were a staple—it might as well have been milk, bread, and patent leather shoes for Mary. White patent leather from Easter through Labor Day, black patent leather for fall and winter. Was that why fifty years later I was still drawn to patent leather?

The old Sanger Harris store in Preston Center had everything I needed—children's clothes, including seasonal patent leather shoes for my girls, and clothes for me. One day I was walking through the handbag department. I saw it, and my eyes locked in on it like laser beams. Yes of course, the purse was patent leather.

Not bright pink patent leather as the saleslady described it. This purse was hot pink and had a hot pink patent leather strap. It was mine before I'd even written the check. I emptied the purse I was carrying right there on the counter and put its contents in my new hot pink patent leather purse. I left carrying my new hot pink patent leather purse. I was proud. I was confident.

Once I got home, I put all my self-help books away. My new hot pink patent leather purse filled all voids of inadequate self-esteem. I felt taller. I felt important. I walked into luncheons and meetings just as Helen Mirren would commandingly walk into a room.

One afternoon, I Helen Mirrened myself into Mom's apartment for a visit, my new hot pink patent leather purse accompanying me. I sat down, as usual, by my mother to visit. She failed to see me because her trained eyes, just as mine had, locked in like lasers on the hot pink patent leather. "Mary, when did you get this wonderful purse?"

"Mom, I bought it recently. Do you like it?" Stupid question as she reached out to fondle the treasure she saw—my new hot pink patent leather purse. My mother had been a beautiful seamstress and loved fashion, always touching or noticing different fabrics or colors I wore. We finally settled down for our visit.

Each time I'd stop in to check on Mom and was carrying my hot pink patent leather purse, she never failed to say how much she liked it. I was slow rather than selfish, I think, but as I was hastily preparing one morning to leave for the day, I picked up my hot pink patent leather purse. Uh-oh, the deep voice. It was God—again: "Mary . . . give . . . your . . . purse . . . to . . . your . . . mother."

My eyes got big. "Okay. Okay, God. I will. Today." Why had I not thought to give my elderly mother my new purse? She loved it and had little to get excited about in her 90s. She'd lost the independence to get out and shop for her own patent leather purse. I knew she'd be happy, but she was beyond happy; she was thrilled beyond measure. Immediately she transferred her few items into her new hot pink patent leather purse, just as I'd done at Sangers.

Mom kept her new acquisition near at all times. She even carried it from her blue chair to the table for meals. If she literally couldn't see her hot pink patent leather purse, which was often, she would frown and ask, "Where's my purse?" It was always within reach.

One day I came by at lunchtime and caregiver shifts were changing. I suggested the four of us go to El Fenix for lunch. My mother would have chosen El Fenix over the Mansion any day of the week. B helped her on her walker, Mom secured her patent leather purse on her arm, and away we went.

We always sat at the same table since it was the quietest, and Mom could hear and participate in the conversation. Twice before our meal was even delivered, she couldn't locate her purse and was reminded it was hanging on the back of her chair. The third time she asked tried my patience, but I lifted it off the chair and assured her that her hot pink patent leather purse was safe.

The fourth time did it. To mask my impatience, I lifted the hot pink patent leather purse up and smilingly said, "Here's your damn purse." My prim and proper mother burst into laughter at my unexpected response as did the caregivers.

Moving from the "missing" purse to the "damn purse" added a silliness to our lunch that made it a delightful and memorable hour. Of course, I repeated my response a couple of times because the comment had gotten such outstanding reception. From that day on, the hot pink patent leather purse became simply the "damn purse" to everyone, especially my mother. The hot pink patent leather purse had given my genteel, soft-spoken, and frustratingly proper mother a confidence and freedom I'd never seen in her.

She changed before my eyes. She mischievously began flinging four-letter words around. "When in the hell is lunch? Where's my damn purse?" She was delighted with herself and in my confusion of new vocabulary. Who was this previously proper lady I'd never heard say "damn?" She had confessed recently that she'd smoked as a young adult but quit when she burned her eyebrows. I began wondering again if there might have been a really fun side of my mother she'd never let us see.

Two and a half months after the death of my mother, I took Beatrice, my mother's faithful caregiver and companion, to the Dallas Arboretum. Beatrice Jones loved flowers, and I knew the 500,000 tulips would enthrall her. The arboretum was a place of beauty and peace that Mother, Beatrice, and I had enjoyed many times in pretty weather. The three of us would take a picnic lunch and eat amid the quiet beauty and serenity of nature. I had a special reason for wanting to make this trip with Beatrice. It was in memory of past times with my mother, and I wanted to give B a gift.

Beatrice and I walked and talked, just the two of us this time. We sat on a rock bench gazing at a sea of pink and white tulips as we ate our lunch, just as we had done when Mother was alive. We spoke of memories the three of us had shared, smiling, laughing at times, and shedding a tear or two. Or I shed the tear or two, not Beatrice. After lunch, I gave B a wrapped gift as a token of love from both Mom and me. She unwrapped her gift and smiled warmly as she looked at me. "Mary, it's the damn purse." B was moved.

Yes, it was—the hot pink patent leather purse my mother had loved, kept within reach, and that had remained a topic of conversation until her death. B and I sat together quietly as she ran her hand lovingly over the hot pink patent leather purse we'd all laughed at so many times. She was quiet as she thought of her friend who was gone.

Those quiet moments with Beatrice were bittersweet with the void of my mother felt deeply by both of us. As B looked inside the purse, she pulled out a card with a note and check of gratitude from my brother and me for everything she'd done for our mother and for us. And for just being Beatrice.

This would have seemed a mundane afternoon to anyone seeing us, but that beautiful spring day held moments of my life as I sat with Beatrice on the stone wall, I shall remember till the day I die. I visualize that intimate scene as if it were yesterday. The sweetness and love, the gentle spring breeze, and the heavenly display of pink and white tulips for B and me signaled the end of a miraculous and beautiful story. Mother was gone, and B and I would not be seeing each other much anymore. Yet the beauty remained that we were two people, sitting side by side, who loved and trusted each other and had walked through my mother's precious life and death together, day after day, year after year.

Mother had told Beatrice one quiet afternoon that B was her best friend. I now took her hand and with my heart full said, "B, you're my best friend too." She was.

10

"I'm Gonna Kick You"

"**W**algreens? That couldn't be! The nursing staff at The Plaza didn't have cough syrup in their medications? Good grief, Patrice! Aren't they taking care of elderly people? I don't care if they are short-staffed on weekends. They're paid to take care of my mother. What is wrong with them?" Sick with fever and a terrible chest cold, my mother could barely breathe because of her constant coughing. On this cold Saturday morning in January, Patrice had the weekend shift for Mother. With grave concern about Mom and getting no help from the staff, Patrice called her grandmother. Beatrice always knew what to do.

"Call Mary immediately." I was in Colorado.

In her worried voice, Patrice told me the situation. "Mary, Mrs. Tompkins is very sick. She can't stop coughing, and the nurse doesn't think it's serious. Grandmama and I do. I insisted the nurse give her something for the cough, so he said he'd go to Walgreens and get some Robitussin." Patrice, like Beatrice, is calm, and if she thought things were not being handled correctly, they weren't. Snow was falling heavily in Colorado where I was living for a few months. With a knot in my stomach, I checked on flights, grabbed a few things, and headed for the airport, deeply grateful Patrice and Beatrice were taking care of a critical situation with Mom when I wasn't there.

By the time I arrived in Dallas, B and Patrice had gotten Mother to the hospital. She was diagnosed with pneumonia which quickly developed into double pneumonia. Mother was 92, and the doctor was not hopeful. This could be the end. My heart sank. As we stood in the hallway talking, Dr. Hominick, who B always called "Dr. Man"—and I never knew where in the world she got that—spoke to me. He put his hand on my shoulder and kindly reminded me, "Mary, none of us is meant to live forever. Your mother is 92 years old." I knew he was right but still, I was sad and scared. You never want to lose your mother. I soon thought if Mother can recover from a subdural hematoma at 90, maybe she can get well from double pneumonia. I'm just glad I, unthinkingly, didn't call Dr. Hominick "Dr. Man" because I'd started using B's name for him a lot. Dr. Hominick never would have understood.

I wanted to comfort my mother as she had comforted me when I was a little girl and got sick. I touched her gentle face and saw her chest moving heavily up and down as she struggled for breath. That was hard to see, but oxygen and sedation began to help. As I comforted Mother, B comforted me. Once again, our team of three hung tight, but Beatrice was the glue.

As Mother got sicker, she became delirious, and B stayed with her day and night. She never left. Vera, Patrice, or Marvella would bring her a change of clothes and anything else she needed. I would come in the mornings, sit with Mom, and talk to Dr. Man and B. If Mom was asleep, B might walk in the halls, and that way, she got to know the nurses. I learned nurses are more attentive to patients whose families are around. B taught me that.

I was worried and sad. My mother was so sick, and I hated seeing her suffer. B and I talked, and that always helped. As we talked softly with Mom sleeping nearby, I was once again reminded of B and my mother speaking softly ten years before in my hospital room after my back surgery. The three of us were still a team, but the patient had changed. Beatrice had become the common denominator of reassurance for my family in serious or critical medical situations.

I sat down with B by the hospital bed. Before I knew it, I smiled, then laughed at a story Beatrice told me that was so funny. It happened earlier that morning. It didn't seem right to get that tickled and even feel lighter with Mother lying ill in the bed so close by, but I couldn't help it the way B told the story.

That morning, while Mom lay resting in bed with her eyes closed, B had quietly begun to give her a bath. "Your mother was delirious, and she opened her eyes and glared at me. She was so mad and told me to leave her alone and get away from her!" Of course, B kept right on gently bathing her patient.

My sweet, gentle but delirious mother then gritted her teeth and said angrily to B, "If you don't quit it, I'm gonna kick you in the face!" My sweet, gentle mother said that?

"Now Mrs. Tompkins, do you think I'm ever gonna put my face where you say you're gonna kick it?" B wasn't intimidated by the threat of a sick, delirious, elderly patient and simply continued the bath. B's down-home wisdom of responding was one of the most endearing attributes of this unique woman.

I was sad for my mom because of the odd behavior delirium

caused, but the way B told the story would have made anyone laugh. That reprieve of unexpected humor helped dilute my sadness the rest of the day. How a 92-year-old woman recovered from double pneumonia, I don't know, but Mom and B were home in eight days. My mother would have adamantly denied she ever said what she did.

After the debacle of the assisted living facility not even having over-the-counter cough syrup for my mother when she was so ill, a general decline of service continued. Mother and B were home from the hospital, but Mom was weak. The pneumonia scare had taken a toll on her. Need for 24-hour care soon became evident.

An apartment would generate significant savings over time, even with adding caregivers at night and on weekends. That would also solve the problem of my complete disgust with the assisted living facility. The only obstacle would be getting Mother's agreement for this move.

My mother did not like change, and I needed her to feel good about a move. I came to discuss this with her during lunch one day. My heart sank as I walked up and saw her sitting in the back of the dining room at a table by herself. Where was B? Then I saw her standing at the edge of the dining area keeping her eye on Mom. "B, why are you not eating with Mother?"

"They don't allow outside caregivers to eat with a patient anymore. Your mother can't see well enough to even cut her food. But I'm watching her." I couldn't believe my ears but went to sit by Mom who looked so alone at her table.

"Hi, Mom, how are you?"

"The food here is terrible." This comment from a woman who rarely complained about anything. The opening was perfect.

"Mom, would you like to move to an apartment?"

"Yes, Mary, I would." My mother has always wanted to think about things for a while—maybe days—before making any decision. Not this time. I was surprised and relieved.

"Guess what, Mom? I've already found a nice apartment close by, and it's a couple of blocks from me. Would you like for me to make a deposit, and you move to this apartment?" Of course, I'd already made the deposit, but it was important Mom felt as if a change that involved her was her decision. That was one reason Beatrice always asked her preferences when appropriate. Wheels were now in motion for another move for Mom and B.

The apartment was perfect—on the first floor with a living room, dining area, kitchen, and bedroom with two east windows. The apartment was cozy yet open and light. Fresh yellow and blue linens soon adorned Mom's new bedroom. Her blue chair, which turned out was the place she basically lived for the next four years, was perfect by the sunny windows. A good friend helped me hang pictures and get the apartment ready. Whenever and wherever Mother moved, B moved.

The day arrived. B and Mom parked in front, and B wheeled Mother to her new apartment. They stopped at the door where Mom, without a word, slowly looked around. She saw family pictures on the wall once again and saw the dining table she'd eaten on as a child. She couldn't quit looking and said, "Mary, this looks like home." That was all I needed to hear. B suggested that she, instead of Patrice, stay with Mom a few nights as Mom adjusted to her new living accommodations.

My mother trusted me with where she lived and felt secure with B. Living in an apartment felt like home, and Mother felt some control seep back into her life. I let her know B would spend the first few nights with her. Discovering this, my mother immediately exerted her new sense of control. "B, I don't want you or anybody else here with me at night. I don't need anybody at night." Mother was firing B, but quick as a wink, B unfired herself.

"That's fine because you'll be asleep and won't even know I'm here." No one, including Mother, ever had answers for B's logic.

Mother and B moved in August, the most miserably hot month in Dallas. August tended to be the month which I've always been involved in a move, and the timing delivered my first dilemma. Before now, B had taken off on holidays since there were nurses in assisted living to check on Mom. Now constant care was needed. Uh-oh, just as I took a breath and thought things were settling down, I realized Labor Day was around the corner. What would I do with B off? I was prepared to make other plans for Mother's care but wondered where in the world I'd find a suitable replacement for one day.

The name of the holiday, Labor Day, signals a break from work—thoughts of escape, fun, being with family, or doing nothing. At the very least, Labor Day is a break from the mundane routine of a job. It's an American holiday.

Since I was now an employer of 24-hour care for my elderly mother, how would future holidays affect the caregivers? I expected Beatrice and her family to be off on Labor Day and other major holidays. They liked getting together for dinner and family gatherings at these times. Of course, these were always at Beatrice's house.

I was tired from the move and did not want another problem. Talking to myself, I reasoned, "All right, Mary, back to Labor Day which needs clarification. You are now running a 24/7 business. It's easy. Deal with this as Beatrice would—directly." So I asked B about her plans for Labor Day and was totally caught off guard with her response.

Beatrice looked at me like I was crazy. "My plans? My plans are to be right here with your mother."

"But B, it's Labor Day, a holiday."

"Yep, sure is. It says 'labor,' don't it? So I guess I'll be laboring. I'll be right here with your mother." Case closed, situation settled, and another window into Beatrice Jones. Her attitude toward life and work kept giving insight into this rare woman.

B arranged the 24-hour shifts. She worked weekdays and filled in anytime one of the others couldn't come. There were early mornings when I'd stop by, and there would be Beatrice. When I'd ask her why she was so early, she'd tell me she spent the night because Vera or Patrice had been unable to come.

The rare times in eight years B was unable to work, she lined up help from her nieces, Saundra and Nicy. I worried for a nanosecond about someone I didn't know taking care of Mother, then realized Beatrice Jones knows exactly what she's doing. I loved both Saundra and Nicy and would have either take care of me if needed.

Life in apartment #142 quickly settled into a comfortable routine. I never worried about the caregivers' schedule because B took care of that. If there were any changes, she let me know. My job was to keep the pantry and refrigerator full, take care of the financial end of things, and make sure all ran smoothly. Most of Mom's and B's time was spent at home except when forays for shopping, the beauty shop and nail salon, or El Fenix became part of their day. They were cute together. B would get Mom settled in the passenger seat of her small car, get herself buckled up, and I always felt a special tenderness seeing the back of their two little heads as they drove away.

Those two became a fixture everywhere. One day as they entered the Vietnamese nail salon by El Fenix, one of the receptionists recognized them as they came in. Because they were always together, she asked cheerily without thinking, "Are the two of you sisters?" Beatrice laughed out loud.

"No, we're not sisters. I help take care of Mrs. Tompkins." Mother's hearing was so poor, she hadn't heard the question. Sisters? One white and one black. My mother would have thought the girl crazy. B thought she was crazy but thought her question was hilarious. Still they were always together, just like close sisters might be.

Occasionally B stayed even two or three days and nights in a row. She might have on the same clothes but never appeared tired or frustrated from staying extra shifts. Her devotion was to my mother first and then her girls if she could help them out.

During cool days of spring, sometimes B wore her Christmas sweatshirt with the large red and green Christmas tree on the front celebrating the Yuletide season. Once she wore this Christmas sweatshirt three days in a row because she'd stayed 72 straight hours with Mom. I was surprised each day seeing B still there in the same sweatshirt. It was that giant red and green Christmas tree that greeted me those three days; then I'd notice the person who wore it.

This time of year, March and April, Dallas women sport happy yellows, pinks, and blues—spring colors. Beatrice Jones had never been affected by fashion mandates of seasonal attire. She just didn't care. Her clothes were clean, and that's all that mattered. B was her own person and knew her patient was what was important. Correct seasonal attire was not.

That's why when spring daffodils were blooming, B looked ready for a frigid, snowy Christmas. That was our B.

11

My Mother and Anne

Life had settled into a predictable routine for Mom and B, so when the breast cancer diagnosis came, it was a shock. B had taken Mom for a mammogram, and the radiologist found a pea-sized tumor in her breast. My mom was diagnosed with breast cancer at age 92. After perfunctory oncology visits, a lumpectomy and six weeks of radiation were scheduled. Two days after the surgery, Mom was home. When I checked on her the following day, I asked how she was feeling. "What do you mean how am I feeling?" was her reply.

"Mom, you had surgery for breast cancer. How are you feeling? Aren't you sore? Look at that big ole bandage covering your entire chest."

"Oh that. Yes, I'm fine." Really? Beatrice and Mom were so alike. Neither showed outward emotion about serious situations. They both dealt with what was in front of them, went on with their days, and often showed surprise when others asked how they were.

My mother had always loved to read. Now confined in old age, there was little for her to do except read, sleep, or visit with B, the kind lady from church who stopped by weekly, and me. Since Mom was blind in one eye and could hardly see out of the other, she was unable to even read large print books anymore. She'd lost interest in television after her brain surgery. With bad hearing and vision, life is severely compromised, especially for the elderly. Mother's eye doctor was a specialist in low vision and had a small, glassed-in room adjacent to his waiting room where equipment could be purchased that would aid patients with exceedingly poor vision.

The reader we bought was the size of a large portable television which greatly magnified print of a newspaper or book. A flat tray was attached below the screen where reading material was placed, and the print was magnified onto the screen. The reader was up there with the blue chair for its inestimable value to my mother. Ability to read on the reader was a godsend because it occupied hours of each day.

When I came in one day after her radiation treatment, Mom was reading her favorite book, *Anne of Green Gables,* and she wanted to continue reading, so I went into the living room to talk to B. She laughed all the time at Mom's copy of *Anne of Green Gables* because sections of the book had come apart since it had been read so much. The incomplete hardback book would be up on the reader with one, two, or three sections of the book on the floor and maybe one in Mom's lap. Mother was now able to read from this larger print copy of the book on her reader. *Anne of Green Gables* was a familiar and loved book from childhood, and Anne, Matthew, Marilla, Mrs. Lynde, and Diana were company for her almost a century after she first read the book.

B would chuckle every time she picked up sections of the

book that had fallen on the floor. Mom knew the story so well that it became "the" book she could get lost in during so many quiet days. She'd read any section within reach. Many hours were passed in pleasure by my mother and Anne while going through breast cancer treatment.

"Why does your mother love this book so much?" B wondered aloud one day. Most people wouldn't really have wanted to know the answer to that, but B did. Her question took me back to my childhood.

"B, I was in third grade and needed to get well to be an angel in the Christmas pageant at school. I was sick in bed with the 'vomiting virus' and felt awful. Mother stayed home from school that week to take care of me. After sips of broth or coke one afternoon, she told me I'd rest better and get well faster if I thought about something else. She sat by my bed and began reading *Anne of Green Gables* in her soothing voice. I fell asleep. When I woke up, I asked her to read more. Anne became our ritual, and I'd forget how badly my tummy hurt as she read. I did get well, but Mother and Anne helped me. By the night of the Christmas pageant, I was well and donned my angel costume as the proudest angel on stage. So B, that's why Mom and I have always had a special bond with Anne. She's loved that book since she was a little girl, and I fell in love with Anne too."

After Mother's brain surgery, I'd purchased that large print copy of *Anne of Green Gables* and brought it to the hospital room as something familiar she might recognize in case she was ever awake enough so I could read to her, just as she had read to me when I'd been sick in third grade. B was satisfied. She liked knowing why my mother loved her book but then looked at me, shook her head, and laughed out loud that I was an angel in the Christmas pageant.

Beatrice would get so tickled at Mom's "go-to" book and chuckle when she'd tell me on the phone that "your mother is reading her book." I still have Mom's well-worn copy of *Anne of Green Gables* on my bookshelf—of course, with a few sections missing.

With my marriage in shambles and other family problems, in June, I escaped to Colorado before I collapsed. B had encouraged me to go, and we kept in touch daily. She took Mom to radiation every day for six weeks. That was a huge burden off of me at a critical time in my life. Beatrice Jones was a salvation in two lives, Mother's and mine.

Mom and B treated radiation as if they were going on a routine errand. The homey oncology building behind Presbyterian Hospital is nestled in a grove of trees with easy parking and punctual appointments. To get to the radiation building, Mom and B had to pass the Jackson Building, the rehabilitation hospital that my mother still hated after three years. She hated even hearing the name.

When Mom had been transferred to the Jackson Building after surgery, she'd not been fully cognizant as her brain injury was ever so slowly healing. She was aware enough to remember what, to her, was bizarre, mean, and unheard-of treatment. The nurses had put restraints on Mom because it was the only way to keep her in bed. She was a high fall risk and would impulsively try to get out of bed because she was unable to process what she could and could not do. One fall could undo the surgery and weeks of healing in her brain, break a hip, result in another brain injury, or be fatal. Finally to keep from putting restraints on her at night, the nurses took her to the piano where they could watch her.

That first morning on the way to radiation, Mom and B passed by the Jackson Building. Mother was a little grouchy, so to tease her out of her mood, B asked, "Mrs. Tompkins, do you want me to drop you at the Jackson Building?"

B was teasing, but any reference to the Jackson Building, Mom took very seriously. "Oh no. Please don't do that," she responded with memories of those terrible days there. B had just discovered gold. This tool of teasing about the Jackson Building, which Mom always interpreted as a sincere question or possibility, was B's most effective way of getting her patient to do something where she was resistant. The dialog was always the same as the first time. "Do you want to go to the Jackson Building?"

"No, I do not." No smile. Mother made an unusually quick switch to cooperative patient.

With a 10:00 radiation appointment each weekday for six weeks, Mom and B were home by 11:00, Mom back reading, and B fixing lunch. I went to the last appointment with both of them, and the doctor told Mom she could scratch breast cancer off her list of worries. Three happy people left radiation that day. I could never have left anyone in charge of my mother's breast cancer treatment at this critical time in her life and my life—except Beatrice Jones. Mom and B took care of what was needed together and made it seem easy.

Apartment #142 was a warm and welcoming place, often with the aroma of a meal being prepared or the washing machine working away. At a difficult time in my life, my mother, in her 90s, and Beatrice, in her 70s, were my support, love, reassurance—and often entertainment.

Being responsible for an elderly parent's life is tiring and hard, but much of life is tiring and hard. The difference is that a loved one is involved. I had one chance to love and honor the mother who had loved and cared for me as only a mother can.

12

Beatrice and Mom
Goin' Fishing

Everything is more serious as one ages, especially in the elderly. I learned a urinary tract infection (UTI) in elderly women can be dangerous, even fatal, if not treated. Because elderly women are often asymptomatic, by the time they are taken to a doctor, the infection is serious, and the patient often requires hospitalization. Confusion and even delirium can set in.

For Mom, her symptoms, which were not really symptoms, were fatigue, disinterest in talking, or just not being alert. Since she had days like this anyway, as we all do, neither B nor I would think much about it. Mom was usually back to herself in a day or two. If she didn't improve after two or three days, that's when B would take her to the doctor. The problem was that you don't run to the doctor every time someone is tired or simply doesn't want to talk.

However, one particular morning, B did take Mom to see "Dr. Man" when she hadn't felt good for several days, and he admitted her to the hospital immediately. She suddenly had become confused, indicative of the critical nature of an elderly UTI. Again B stayed all day and all night while Mom was in the hospital.

While we were in the ER waiting to be admitted, the nurse began hooking up IVs and preparing to move Mom to a room. I was standing on one side of her bed and B on the other. The nurse told Mother she needed to remove her rings while in the hospital. "No! I've had this ring on since my wedding day! I'm not taking it off! My other ring was my daddy's diamond pendant! You can't take these!" B and I glanced at each other across the bed. What was going on? Mother's wedding day had been 70 years before, and yes, she'd had her ring off before, but to Mom, her wedding ring had never left her finger. She was angry and adamant—a bad combination.

I had to think fast and pulled a trump card. I had two. I looked at Mother and calmly asked, saying each word slowly and clearly making sure she heard. "Mom, do you trust me?" I waited. She slowly turned her head and looked squarely at me with her pretty, stubborn brown eyes. B was silent, the nurse was silent; everywhere was silence. Would there be an upsetting scene over this situation or not?

Then Mother answered quietly. "Yes, Mary, I do." I looked over at B and let out a big breath of air. I had asked a chancy question of someone sick, confused, and on the verge of delirium, but the answer was lucid. I realized later what a sweet moment that had been in the ER with so much going on around us—blood withdrawal, the nurse taking vitals, and the doctor asking questions. But I heard none of that. The gift of trust from my mother at that moment was worth everything.

I understood her wedding ring and her father's diamond pendant that she'd made into a ring were visible ties to the two men she loved most, and taking them off felt as if her bond to them would be broken. I assured her the minute she came home, I'd bring her rings over. Mom looked down, removed her rings, and handed them to me.

One could have observed several interactions and personalities that summer afternoon in the ER. Something I didn't think of until later was the realization that no matter what Beatrice's opinions were, never did she offer advice or try to persuade or override me when I was interacting with or making decisions that concerned my mother. B, Mom, and I shared a mutual respect and trust for each other.

Once Mother was taken to a room, sweet Beatrice told me to go home, and she'd call me if I was needed. She knew I was tired. B and Mom were just about settled in "their" room, and nurses were taking blood pressure and reading her chart again.

The following day when I came in, Mom was sleeping, B was standing by her bed, and as I sat down, she began chuckling. I knew then she might have a story about Mom, but how could something be funny in this serious situation? Then I remembered B had made me laugh before during times when Mother had been ill.

Why wouldn't something be funny with Beatrice in charge? She delighted in the eccentricities of people of any age. When she started laughing, which she usually did before one of her stories, I half-smiled and gave B my full attention. That day, I wondered what could have been funny with a sleeping patient and quiet nurse. "Mary, I've got a story 'bout your mother." But she began chuckling before she could tell her story.

Earlier my sick mother had waked from a nap, looked right at B, and said, "B, let's get out of here and go fishing. You just put me in that wheelchair and wheel me out. I've got a fishing pole. Come on. Let's go." My mother might have fished as a child but not as an adult. In my whole life, I'd never even heard her speak of fishing. The delirium was concerning and, obviously, still present, yet humor in the midst of a serious situation is a balm that can temporarily settle the heart and mind. Thank you, Beatrice, for telling me these stories and being my mom's fishing buddy.

Once the UTI was gone, Mom and B were, once again, back in #142, and life went fairly smoothly for the next two years. Occasional visits from out-of-town family and the weekly visit from the kind lady at church were the only company Mom had. My children were in their 20s and busy starting their lives but visited their grandmother when they could. Most of Mom's friends had died. Without B, my mother would have been very lonely.

By the end of those two years, Mother was 94 years old and Beatrice was 75 and still going strong. How she did this, I will never know because B had her own serious health issues, one being diabetes. Beatrice took care of her medicine and diet so naturally, I'd forget she had this disease until late one afternoon. I was sitting on the sofa chatting with her before I left. She missed something I said and then didn't respond when I asked her a question. B's eyes weren't focusing either. Something was wrong. Now I needed to nurse the nurse!

What was wrong, and what do I do? Should I call an ambulance? Since Patrice was on her way for her night shift, I tried her before calling 911. She answered right away, and I told her what was going on. "Mary, Grandmama's blood sugar is way down. She needs some sugar. I'm almost there. Get her to drink some orange juice right away." As I poured the juice, I wondered how I'd handle things if B refused to drink the juice since she wasn't fully cognizant. I was having to think like Beatrice. However, she didn't refuse. She sipped the juice and after a few sips looked at me and asked what I was doing. I told her what had happened. Patrice walked in that minute and walked straight to her grandmother.

"Grandmama, your blood sugar was low. That's what happened. Mary gave you some orange juice. How do you feel?"

After pausing a minute, B looked at us. "I feel fine. I just needed a little juice."

"B, you scared me."

"Scared you? Good grief, Baby. I'm fine, so you don't need to go making a fuss over me."

"B, will you always make sure you drink your juice on time?"

"I will. I just got busy and forgot. Let me sit here for a few minutes, and then I'm going home."

The day ended with B recovered, but Patrice being on time and walking in when she did, taught me what to do if this were to happen again to B or someone else with diabetes. I learned from reading that people with diabetes often cannot feel a sudden blood sugar drop, which B hadn't. If she hadn't gotten sugar into her system, her body could have gone into diabetic shock. It was amazing how quickly a few sips of juice gave her the sugar her body craved. I left thinking I needed to sign up fast for a first aid course.

For the next few days, B would get tickled and when I asked why, she'd say, "You two were funny stewing all around me. I was fine."

"B, you were not fine, and I was scared."

"Well, I'm fine now." There was nothing more to say to this woman who is so used to having diabetes, as well as, ending a conversation. B knew not to panic, but I didn't. In addition to diabetes, B had a history of terribly high blood pressure and heart problems. She stayed on schedule with her medicine and saw her doctors regularly. Once again, Beatrice dealt with what she had to and continued to live life with zest. Seventy-five years old with serious health issues, and she still worked a full week and sometimes more—alert and energetic.

By the end of these relatively calm two years, Mother began to have more and more health problems. She'd lost almost all of her vision and hearing; she had atrial fibrillation but could not have any more cardioversions; she'd begun having small strokes, transient ischemic attacks (TIAs); and UTIs became critical before we knew it. Even kindly Dr. Man said he couldn't do any more for Mother—to take her to the emergency room if medical attention was needed. There were no more permanent fixes.

After days of debating the pros and cons, I picked up a very heavy phone and called hospice. I expected a somber voice on the other end of the phone. Instead, the woman was cheery but sincere as I told her Mom's situation. She assured me I was not overreacting by contacting them. "If it would be convenient for you and your mother, we could come out and assess her this afternoon. We would then let you know if we would be suitable help for her." An afternoon visit was scheduled.

Again B didn't question my decision to seek additional help or worry her job was in jeopardy. She was exactly what I expected—supportive. Some LVNs might have felt their position as caregiver demeaned by calling in another source for help—not B. She wanted the best for my mother, she knew her worth, and she knew my job was to see my mother had the very best care possible.

The hospice nurse spoke to B and me after her assessment. "Your mother absolutely qualifies for our help if you decide. My best estimate, and it's only an estimate, is that she has about six more months. If you do decide, this is how we would proceed. I would come out to check her once or twice a week. The social worker would come once a week, and our chaplain would stop in two to three times a week. There wouldn't be any more hospital visits. If she were to develop a UTI or another situation comes up, I'll come and treat her right here. Why don't you think about it and see if you'd like us to start." I didn't have to think about it.

"How soon could you begin?" The nurse, social worker, and chaplain came two days later for Mom's first official hospice visit. Three years later, hospice was still coming by for the woman who was supposed to live only six months. Mother and Beatrice were two tough women.

The nurse had been efficient and nice. She wasn't in the least bit somber like "this is the end." She was friendly yet professional, kind but direct. Her manner with Mother was comfortable, like a friend, as she took her vital signs and chatted with her. I realized we would only be adding to the team of Beatrice and her girls, not creating confusion. No more hospital or ER for UTIs? That was a godsend.

Instead of being sad at having hospice involved with Mother, I was reassured. I wanted to do all I could for my mother, just as she'd done for her mother and just as B had done for her parents. I was clear this meant not only providing the best care possible but being part of Mom's life on as much of a daily basis as I could. Visits without being in a hurry, not just calls and "how are you's." She didn't choose to be dependent on others. Life did that. She was my mother who had loved me every day of my life, and now the roles had changed. It was my turn to step in and show her how much I loved her—that she was every bit as important as she'd always been. This was how B treated the sick and the elderly. Time is a worthy sacrifice.

When the hospice nurse came, she would tell B and me, or just B, what she'd seen that day. Beatrice was grateful for her observations and input, and the nurse was grateful for information B passed along. Jim, the kind and compassionate chaplain, began coming three times a week. The nurse and Jim gave Mother company besides B and me. Both Mom and B had some deep conversations with Jim. If I wasn't there, B would relay any pertinent information—and there was often a story.

Quickly, the times with B, my mother, the nurse, and chaplain became a social hour. I'd often hear gales of laughter from inside before I opened the door. Apartment #142 became the party place for this hospice team to share the joy of everyday life with B and Mom. For a while, Mother seemed to improve rather than decline. Hospice said they would just keep coming. I'd always thought hospice was used in only critically ill and imminent death situations. Not so.

Hospice marveled at my mother's resilience. Beatrice, the hospice nurse, and Jim, the chaplain, delighted in my mother's selective hearing. If a compliment was sent her way, she could hear. If B or I told her it was time for something she didn't want to do, she couldn't hear. The nurse would compliment Mother on her strong constitution, and Mom would smile, exceedingly pleased with herself. Hospice was a wonderful blessing and support for Mom, B, and me.

The hospice crew often stayed longer than their allotted social hour. They liked coming to Mom's and kept it up for three years. I think Mom and B were, maybe, a respite for sad situations with which they dealt. Mom's six-month prognosis had come and gone. Beatrice and Jim, the chaplain, had become fast friends, having spiritual talks and trading war stories. I now felt I'd hired a companion for Beatrice.

13

"Be Hearing 'bout That"

Mother's vision had declined so dramatically that she could no longer even read on her reader. All the pieces of *Anne of Green Gables* were put aside. Mom sat quietly or slept in her blue chair or talked with B or me, or B and me. Times became quieter. Mom and B had conversations I never knew about, some light, some serious.

My mother didn't want to burden me with things she worried about. She talked to B. This way I could tell Mom about her grandchildren or what I was doing or that I was fine—that's what she needed to hear and loved best from me. Knowing what was going on in my life or my children's lives made her feel included. If I had on a blouse, shirt, or pants that she could tell was a soft fabric, she'd feel it. Once I had on a fleece jacket. As she rubbed her hand lightly back and forth on the fleece, she said softly, "Mary, this feels like a bird." B and I smiled at this sweet, innocent, and childlike comment.

Mom's love and interest in fabrics never diminished. B

would get tickled when Mom would inspect the seams of clothes at "Draper and Diamond" or comment on clothes my girls or I had on. She absolutely loved when our 94-year-old fashion consultant told Jenny that her skirt was too short. B understood people. She understood the interests of my mother, and this served to deepen the relationship between the two.

Since Mom couldn't read anymore, she had time to pursue her hobby—worrying. She often worried about me, a lifelong habit, but she'd talk to B who would listen and say something reassuring to allay Mom's concerns. My mother had always been smarter and savvier than I gave her credit for. She quietly took in the flow of conversations, feelings she got around others, and assessed many situations accurately. I'd find that out later and was always surprised.

Many times I had no idea Mom was even aware of what was going on because she really didn't participate in conversations since she couldn't hear. Hearing loss leaves people out of the world in which they live and formerly participated in. This is sad, but for Mom, she enjoyed being around family, listening, and observing.

There was one Christmas morning she hadn't enjoyed. Mom's silent radar was on high alert as she accurately assessed a tense family situation. We'd always had Mom over on Christmas morning, and now the bonus was Beatrice coming with Mom. Out of four children, two were working, one was married, and one was in college. The den was full—grown children, my husband and me, and Mother and Beatrice. The abundance of gifts under the Christmas tree had been passed out and opening began.

Intuitively known or naively unknown to me, these were the last days of my marriage. There was tension in the room that I masterfully covered, or so I thought. I got through the excessive gift giving with wrapping paper strewn over the floor. Shouldn't a scene like that have been the Norman Rockwell image of a joy-filled Christmas morning with family, lights on the tree, Christmas music playing, and a blazing fire in the fireplace? I'd tried my best to make it so, especially around Mom and B, but no success. B told me later that when she and Mom got in B's little gray car to go home, my mother had turned to her and said, "There's trouble in that household." I was stunned. She knew, and B was the one she was safe to talk to.

After a six-month separation, finally the blinders came off. I'd been swimming laps in the pool at the gym. In the middle of a lap, I fully and finally comprehended the state of my marriage. I stopped, stood up, and admitted to myself that my greatest dream—that of a happy marriage and walking into the sunset with a best friend was not to be. The marriage was over. It had been imploding for years. I was in the middle of a swimming pool safe and sound but realized I'd been drowning with no water around for years. I went home and removed my wedding ring. It was past time to deal with real life, not a fantasy life.

Several days later at Mom's apartment, she and I were visiting. I held her hand, and she put her other hand on top of mine, a sweet gesture. Or so I thought. My mother could be cagey. Her fingers patted my hand but then moved over my fingers, stopped on my ring finger, and felt. They felt again, right where I'd worn my wedding ring. Good grief. Was my elderly mother turning into a private investigator? I looked up at B questioningly, and she mouthed, "I'll be hearing 'bout that." B knew what had been going on with my marriage even though I didn't speak of it. She just knew. She did know of the separation and knew, probably by my demeanor, it wasn't working. I had not wanted to upset my mother by talking about any of this.

I wanted to get in my car and just drive north, maybe to the North Pole. B would care for Mom, my children were grown, and I could escape life. But I didn't. A few days later when I came by to check on Mom, B nodded "yes" as I came in. I closed the door. "Yep, she asked why you didn't have your ring on. I tried to assure her that you would be all right." Beatrice Jones was a godsend once again.

B took care of Mom in so many ways. I assured Mom I was fine. That's what she needed to know—nothing except that her little girl, then 58, was doing fine. That wasn't true, but it would be one day. B was there to listen when Mother's worries appeared, and appear they did. A trusted friend who would listen, understand, and respond wisely to Mother was a blessing.

These dark years of my life occurred simultaneously with my mother's rapidly declining health and the addition of hospice. I didn't talk to Mom about dying. I just couldn't at that time. I knew she wanted to be buried in Dallas, and that was enough. I knew my mom and knew she thought about her death, of course, but those are the conversations she had with Beatrice and Jim, the two most comforting people she could have around.

Mom and I both knew her time would come. We'd gone through the slow death of my father and picking out a casket together. I knew how to pick out a casket but didn't want to do that by myself. Just as in B's family, there had been many deaths and funerals in my extended family. I don't regret not having these conversations with Mother because she needed what I gave her and needed what B gave her. Maybe from me, that was just love and being there. Did we not have to talk about her impending death because we both knew it was already settled within each of us? I think so.

After the initial estimate from hospice of six months left for Mother, I made another difficult call—this time to Sparkman Hillcrest, the funeral home and cemetery where Mother wanted to be buried. Having basic plans in place would make things simpler and less chaotic upon my mother's death. She had been blessed with a long and good life. She was 96 years old. She would die. We all knew that and didn't need to talk about it. Plus Mom had survived so many illnesses; maybe she'd outlive us all.

I didn't want to do this, making plans at a funeral home for someone, a few blocks away, who was probably involved in a pleasant conversation with Jim or B. I felt I was going behind her back. B reminded me I'd been going behind her back for years. I had been making decisions for my mother's welfare when she was unable to, but the way B said I'd "been going behind her back for years" was funny. B was just putting a fact out there of what we have to do at times.

That interchange lightened the moment, but all of a sudden, we both thought of the same situation at the same moment. We remembered when we'd cleared out all those clothes from Mother's closets—the clothes with the million shiny safety pins. I suppose our actions might have been duplicitous since Mom continued for years to berate the selfish, mysterious thief who'd stolen all her clothes. But now, B and I got so tickled, all over again, as we remembered those two unbelievable days, "behind her back," we had spent in Mom's closets.

How many memories B and I shared together. As always, laughter gave perspective and laughing with B even more perspective. Now the dreaded appointment with Sparkman

Hillcrest seemed almost normal. For B, making funeral plans was just another errand. She told me she'd already paid for her funeral because she didn't want any of her family saddled with having to pay her expenses. Beatrice had always earned her own money and paid her own way, including the end of her life.

On a hot August morning, I parked by a line of squeaky-clean black Cadillacs at Sparkman Hillcrest. There I was again, planning a transition in August, which ensured the most misery possible from Dallas summer heat and which did seem to burn down on me that day as I inspected gravesites. I was choosing where my mother would one day be buried.

So many questions: how many plots did I want to purchase, how much did I want to spend, and where did I want the plots? I had no idea of the answers. I'd never had shopping for burial plots on my weekly to-do list. I saw huge headstones with family names and 10 or 15 graves or grave sites laid out and enclosed by low walls. I didn't have a family dynasty to plan for, so I decided Mom would be pleased if I bought a plot for the two of us next to each other. What difference does it make if you're all buried together or not? "You won't know. You're dead." B's logic. Uh-oh. I'm beginning to think like Beatrice.

I told B my father was buried in Corpus Christi in a large "Tompkins" family plot with his parents, his five brothers and their wives, and who knows who else. My cousins still call and tell me to "come to Corpus because there's plenty of room for you and your kids." Daddy had always told Mom, "I'm going to be buried in Corpus. I hope you'll come with me." Daddy got his wish but Mom had a different one. B had smiled at that conversation between my parents. She loved hearing our family stories just as we loved hearing hers.

I made another decision—I wanted Mom and me to be

near grass and trees, if affordable. The thought of my mother and, eventually, me being laid to rest in a quiet setting gives me peace even today. I also had the naive thought that dying is a sad time, so it doesn't seem right to charge someone to die. The woman kept looking at her price sheet.

The first place we looked was lovely and had the comforting sound of a fountain in the background. What was not comforting was the noise from traffic nearby. These particular plots were separated from Northwest Highway by an ivy-covered iron fence. Lovely location but oh, so noisy. The last location, the Rose Garden, was the one: peaceful with green grass surrounding the graves and gravesites. The nice young woman showed me a row of eight plots. "No thank you. I just need two." These two plots would soon be under the shade of a lovely, large oak tree. No noise. And Neiman Marcus could be seen in the distance.

We will all die, just like B said. I realized elderly people aren't living a life they'd ever choose anyway, but Mother and Beatrice set the bar high by accepting aging and its unwelcome changes with grace and dignity, most of the time.

A repeat of so many Beatrice and Mary conversations occurred the day after I was at Sparkman Hillcrest. Updating B on my appointment there, I mentioned I hadn't wanted Mother buried in the plot with the fountain by Northwest Highway because the traffic was so noisy.

"Yep, that traffic would sure bother your mother, wouldn't it?" I momentarily paused and then burst out laughing at B— and myself. Beatrice Jones can get to the bottom line faster than anyone I've ever known. As always, B and I could see the comedy in nothing—this time in a burial plot. She helped me see humor in situations that weren't humorous, and I loved that about her. Ability to do this enables one to have perspective and get through hard times more easily. I love B's aspect of humor but have to be careful with whom I share my aberrant insights.

My mother would have gone with me to the funeral home had she been able. Beatrice would have been with us too. Then we would have gone to El Fenix for lunch.

Beatrice Jones

Beatrice in younger days

Beatrice and N.D. Wedding Day

Mother and Beatrice having a Merry Christmas

Beatrice and Mom going to Mother's Day Brunch

The Day of the Red Convertible

Beatrice and family on Patrice's Graduation Day

Beatrice and Kyisha

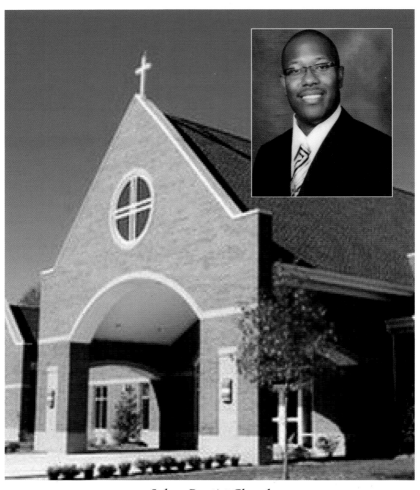

Salem Baptist Church,
Pastor Todd Atkins—B's grandson

*Beatrice at Dallas Arboretum inheriting the
pink purse after Mother's death*

Beatrice and Mary at Salem Baptist Church

Beatrice's 84th birthday

Giving Beatrice my tribute to her

14

"I'm Calling the Police!"

Confirmation that Mother knew she was nearing the end of her life occurred one evening when my brother, Danny, was in town to see Mother. Danny had always added a spark to Mother's life whether he was on the phone or coming to visit. He was the glorified first son, six years older than I, and my only sibling. He is now "Dan" to friends and business colleagues, but to family, he'll always be Danny. My parents, Danny, and I grew up in a small duplex in Houston when life was a lot simpler. Danny drove me crazy, and he was my hero.

Once he left for graduate school in California, he never missed Mom's birthday or mine—and that's been over 50 years. He always sent Mom flowers and both Mom and me a birthday card. B, Mom, and I loved Danny's birthday cards every year because they were always FedExed. He was busy doing deals in the Silicon Valley but still took time to buy cards and write a personal note as well as call. By the time this savvy dealmaker had paid decades of FedEx charges, he probably could have taken a trip around the world, but birthdays wouldn't have been the same for us. FedEx was part of his gift. B called or said every year when I came by, "Your mom's FedEx from your brother came a while ago," and she'd just chuckle. B understood so many nuances of our family dynamics.

Since Beatrice cared for my mother for almost ten years, she and I had a chance to have many and varied conversations and experiences. Danny had conversations with B, too, when he came to visit Mom, and he, occasionally, had lengthy conversations from California with her when he'd call. He'd never admit it, but he liked to bend Beatrice's ear and get her take on various subjects and situations. She was entertaining and savvy. Danny has a great sense of humor and loved B's directness and at times, blunt answers. Suffice to say, Danny knew Beatrice well. Her care and compassion for our mother as well as her sense of humor, common sense, and faithfulness endeared her to my brother, my children, my cousins, and my good friends.

One day Danny laughed and confessed, "You know, Mary, Beatrice is really something. She has an answer for everything, and you know, she's usually right." His raucous laugh, as he'd simultaneously slap his right thigh, could be heard a block away and was so characteristic of him. Danny respected B's directness and brand of wisdom as much as anyone he knew. This from my brother who thought he knew everything about everything.

A time when Danny was here, not too many months before Mother's death, B had fixed us all dinner. The four of us enjoyed a relaxing time together at the table. B cleaned the kitchen while Mom, Danny, and I kept talking. A lull in the conversation was Mom's perfect opening. She turned to her son: "Danny, I want to talk to you." What a highly unusual statement from Mother, at her age. At this moment, she became the parent speaking. All three of us were surprised.

I was Danny's ride home, so I couldn't leave. B was sitting on the sofa, out of sight, but heard Mom trying to scoot her chair around, and she and Danny got up to help; B instinctively knew when she could help. Mom now sat at a 90-degree angle to the table, and Danny turned around to face her. They sat facing each other in straight back chairs just a few feet apart. The way the chairs were set up looked like preparation for a mini FBI interrogation. Seeing this setup with the two would have been funny had my mother not been so intent. Whatever this was, it was highly important to Mother.

Mom sensed that this could be Danny's last visit before she was gone and wanted to talk to him. She needed to put final pieces of her life in place. Everything was quiet. B and I would hear the conversation because Mom's apartment was small, but neither Danny nor Mother seemed to care.

My brother kindly and respectfully asked, "Mom, what do you want to talk about?" There was a pause.

"Danny . . . do you have a job?" Mom asked this question in a calm, confident voice. No question could have surprised my brother more, me more, and Beatrice more. Danny hadn't been without a job since he was 11 years old with a paper route. He was taken aback at the question but knew Mom was deadly serious. To see my 96-year-old elderly mother in charge of a conversation with her adult son was incredibly sweet, as was Danny's doing anything he could to help put her at ease. I looked over at B. Not a sound from her, but she was bent over double, her head in her lap and her shoulders shaking because she was laughing so hard.

Why were Danny and I so taken off guard at Mom's question and B so tickled? Because everyone, and I mean everyone, knew Danny was a major workaholic. This guy was born doing deals, and even when we were young, Danny would try to cut deals with me when I was a mere seven years old and asked to ride his bike. He'd had jobs in college and then worked to pay his way through graduate school. The boy had his faults, but one thing he always had was a job.

Danny loved his mother and respected her need to ask whatever it was she needed to know. They looked right at each other, and his brief moment of surprise barely showed as he answered her question of having a job. "Yes, Mom, I do. I have a pretty good job." I smiled at his answer.

Mother had always known about her son's work, his drive and ambition, and his successes. Had she forgotten? Was it dementia? Or was her question that of a dying woman who needed reassurance that what she cared most about in life was in order?

Mom was ready for her next question. "Danny, will you see that Mary is taken care of?" What? Was I still the little sister who needed him to beat up the neighborhood bully for pushing me over on my bike? No, I was not! I was an independent woman who could take care of herself, and if need be, I'd get a job. I momentarily bristled but quickly realized this was a dying mother's need to know that both her children would be fine, no matter their age. Mother knew I'd traded in a career to raise children and that I was no longer married, although we had never used the d-word. This might have been the root of her question.

She still saw her son as the big brother who would watch out for me, whether it was beating up bullies in the neighborhood, pumping me to ballet on his bike, or teaching me to play football and baseball; the fact is I will always be the little sister. A dying woman pulled forth the strength of a mother's heart as her last gift of love to Danny and me.

Beatrice was still bent over double guffawing silently at

her total surprise at Mom's assertive, parental questioning of her son. B knew Danny and I were both capable of taking care of ourselves, but she also had been totally taken off guard by her dying patient's change, at age 96, from elderly mother into "I'm-in-charge" parent.

Danny responded to Mom's question of would he "take care of" me by kindly saying what she needed to hear. "Yes, Mom, I will do that." It was quiet. "Mom, is there anything else you'd like to talk about or ask me?"

"No, that is all." Mom was satisfied. She could now relinquish her parental role and return to elderly mother role. Her questions had been answered. This five-minute conversation was tender, funny, sad, beautiful, memorable . . . and a goodbye. I was proud of both my mother and brother at that moment— my mother for mustering the courage and energy to ask what she needed to know and my brother for showing the love he had for his mother in the kind and understanding way he did. Once again, having B there gave perspective and normalcy. B loved and understood our mother so well.

Following his interrogation, Danny helped Mom back on her walker, and I went in to talk to B. I couldn't talk to her because she was still laughing her head off at the scene that had just occurred. I'd seen B tickled at Mom but never like this.

Danny flew back to California, hospice still came, and Mom and B continued with their days. We all knew Mother's life was quickly ebbing away. Yet the mood in apartment #142 remained positive with B and Jim there, whose presence was a great comfort to my mother. Mom became even quieter and didn't have much to say when I came by but was always glad to see me.

With Mom talking less, we often just sat and held hands. She knew I was there and knew B was there. Mom was almost

97 now, and she slept more and more in her blue chair. She would hold hands with B at times and neither would talk. The quiet was their conversation.

Even during this time, when the days of my mother's life were numbered, there were stories of B and Mom. One afternoon, I was privileged to see the tenderest moment I'd seen in Beatrice's and Mother's relationship. B and I were by Mom's blue chair chatting quietly with her. Mother closed her eyes, which she sometimes did before saying something important, and slowly turned her head to B who was standing to her right. She slowly lifted her right hand and placed it on B's left forearm. She looked right up at Beatrice, and I heard her soft but sure voice: "B . . . you're my best friend." Mother, again, was saying something she needed to say before she died. I teared up.

At that moment, Mother and B became the exact replica of Miss Daisy and Hoke in *Driving Miss Daisy*. Mom and Miss Daisy, two strong women and both dedicated schoolteachers, had to be dependent on another for care and companionship in their last years. Their statements of "Hoke, you're my best friend" and "B, you're my best friend" were recognition of the faithful care, love, and loyalty extended to each for years.

Life can be comforting when you have a best friend, but even so, there are occasional blips. One morning Beatrice was definitely not Mom's best friend. B had awakened her twice to get up, get a bath, and eat breakfast. Mom didn't want to get up, get a bath, and eat breakfast. She wanted to sleep. The third time B woke her, Mother's stubbornness kicked in.

"Mrs. Tompkins, you need to get up. It's time for your bath, and you need to eat breakfast. Time to get up now." My mother was adamant she didn't want to get up, get a bath, and eat breakfast and resisted again. "Mrs. Tompkins, it's 10:00.

I've let you go back to sleep twice. We are going to get up, and I am going to give you a bath."

Turning her head to B, Mom threatened, "I'm calling the police!" Where my mother's response to B came from, I'll never know because it was not like the mild-mannered mother I was used to. But she'd finally had it with being told what to do. A nanosecond passed.

"Okay, I'll hand you the phone. You call the police, but you can't even see those big ole numbers on the phone Mary got you." In that situation, I would have kindly coaxed my mother. Not Beatrice. She was herself. She kindly, but matter-of-factly, let my mother know, she might be dying, but she was not in charge.

The white flag appeared. Mom was defeated and knew it; she tried hard not to be tickled at B's reply, but she couldn't help it. They chuckled together. B had made my mother laugh at herself so many times over the years. Mom had her bath and ate her breakfast, and the day continued as usual.

I cannot imagine my life or my mother's life without Beatrice Jones. She was family. Beatrice was the best thing that ever happened to Mother and me in the last decade of my mother's life.

B's consistent professionalism, work ethic, and compassion outweighed anything I have ever seen or will see. Add to that wisdom, common sense, and a quirky and delightful sense of humor. Mother and *Anne of Green Gables* both found their kindred spirit: Mother in her dying days and Anne in her childhood, Mother not looking and Anne seeking. Mother found Beatrice and Anne found Diana.

15

The Pit

S*ui generis* is a Latin phrase meaning "of its own kind." I laughed out loud when I read that phrase because it described Beatrice Jones perfectly with her unique brand of wit and wisdom. Each member of her family agrees. Everyone who knew Beatrice was drawn to her. They loved her sense of humor and down-home way of speaking. People came to her for advice because she always had a solution laced with wisdom. They listened to her. I have. My mother has. My assertive brother has. Beatrice's children, grandchildren, great-grandchildren, and great-great-grandchildren have.

Beatrice Dilworth Jones had an answer to anything and everything. Her responses were instantaneous and succinct. Her solutions made sense and seemed to be right, or at the very least, they were for her. If anyone did not agree with her, she didn't care. One thing for certain: there was never hesitancy in a response from B. Never.

Beatrice carried this trait within her family, with patients,

patients' families, friends in and outside of church, and neighbors. What you saw was what you got. No surprises. Her responses reminded me of a definition of wisdom I once heard from a New York minister: "Wisdom is looking at the world realistically and making the right decision most of the time. It's beyond morals." This fit Beatrice Jones perfectly.

Beatrice was the wise one I'd call when the pain of divorce got too heavy. She'd listen, and there were no one-sentence answers then. Her response was bottom-line though. She spoke slowly and lovingly to me one night. "Baby, they're pushin' you in The Pit. Let 'em do their whatever, but don't let anybody put you there in that pit with 'em. I don't know why they would treat you that way, but we don't wanna be like those 'poor me' folks. I tell peoples sometimes, 'You talkin' like sick folks.' There's no one down in that pit to help you out. You gotta climb out yourself." That's what Beatrice had done so many times in her life, and she'd learned how. The way she described "The Pit" gave me a visual of an awful, sewage-filled, deep, filthy hole. No one wants to be there! I didn't want to be there! But B made sense, in her unique way, as to why I was stuck in my life. I was in The Pit. I needed to get out. Fast.

I ended up laughing and asked, "Okay B, but *how* do I get out of The Pit?" My pit was pretty dang deep.

"Well . . . you kick a little dirt off the side, then put your foot in there, grab above, and just start climbin' out. Then kick more dirt, put your foot in again and keep a' climbin'. That's how. Each step you're gettin' closer. That's what ya' gotta do. Pretty soon you'll be out." Nothing has ever sounded so ridiculous and so wise at the same time, but by then, I was listening intently, and I believed every word of what she said. There was no doubt in B's mind what my problem was. She'd been there. I was getting what I'd thought impossible—a specific solution.

I had to get out of that filthy pit! It is an awful place. I decided I'd start kicking and climbing right then.

The Pit is a visual I keep in my arsenal. My pit was deep, and B's advice turned into the hardest work I've ever done in my life. The Pit is a bad place to be, and, no matter what, I'm determined to never go back there. Thank you, Beatrice Jones, for being my advocate.

Another time, B gave me another way to avoid The Pit. She remembered back to when she'd had a slew of bad days and "sure as shootin'" was near The Pit. "Mary, when I get anywhere near that pit, I march to the front door, I open it, and I say loud, 'Get out Satan! Get out now!' I slam that door hard to make sure he's gone. Then I lean against the door so he can't open it, and I catch my breath. After a minute, I feel better." That was B's practical Christianity at work. I'd smiled at B, but that was her solution, and it worked for her. Why not try it? I had a front door. Pretty simple, pretty practical. Another tool in my arsenal for The Pit.

Through the years, in both Mom's and my conversations with B, I began jotting on scraps of paper, napkins, or torn pieces of newspaper, some of B's sayings that could address daily life, a belief, or complex life problem. I called my compilation of these "The Wit and Wisdom of Beatrice Jones."

B usually didn't volunteer her advice, but if you asked, you'd better be ready. She would give it. B's simple but practical advice confirmed my definite belief in the absolute existence of The Pit. The following are a few of Beatrice's colorful takes on various subjects edited from "The Wit and Wisdom of Beatrice Jones:"

Response when she was feeling a little sluggish, and I'd asked, "B, how're you doing?" "Steppin' not fast, kickin' not high."

Dead flowers: "Those flowers done bowed their heads."

Payday: "I call Friday 'Happy Day.' It's the day you get paid."

Heaven and hell: "You better be good. There's no exit in hell."

Complainers saying "if only" this or that had happened or been done: "I've never seen 'if only' doing anything!"

Someone or something old: "Older than black pepper."

Rain: "The devil's beatin' his wife."

Someone complaining about being the black sheep of the family: "Well, I guess you are if that's what you decided on."

Why she doesn't speak in front of a group: "When I stands up, my voice sits down."

A colorful blouse: "A top that smiles."

Prayer: "Pray ahead of time so when you get sick, you don't have to hurry up and pray."

Alcohol: "Ignorant oil."

Alcoholics in a family: "Well, everybody's got some Bubba's and Lucy's in their family."

An illegitimate baby: "That child ain't illegitimate. Those parents are illegitimate!"

Parents complaining about children: "You had fun layin' down makin' 'em. Now stand up and raise 'em."

Marriage: "You don't have trust, you don't have a marriage."

When something valuable breaks: "If something breaks, it's gone, and when you're gone you don't come back."

A break-in at her home: "Well, I guess God didn't think I needed all that jewelry."

Death: "You might as well get ready because people are gonna die. I know my heart is right so I'm not worried. When I go in that ground, I won't know it because I'll be dead. I came in this world alone, and I'll leave alone."

A wheelchair: "Don't get in that wheelchair. Once you get

in a wheelchair, you'll never get out. It's okay if ya' walk slow. Just keep walkin'."

There is so much that encompasses this woman for such a seemingly simple person. Beatrice has never sought attention for herself. She has given and served others her entire life. That's who she is. Beatrice Jones is one of those rare people who won't get attention from the world but who makes the world a better place. She takes life one day at a time. She is full of gratitude for every little thing she has, including warm water.

B had no need ever to defend herself because she was confident in her own skin. She knew who she was. She was neither better nor worse than another. She loved freely and gave freely. She did not hold onto things that didn't matter. Her stolen jewelry was an example.

Beatrice spoke her mind when appropriate, and anyone would have known where she stood. She laughed. She loved. At 82, B still had great-grandchildren and great-great-grandchildren dropped off at her house for her to watch while the parents worked, and she still kept them in line. B and I were on the phone one day, and she said abruptly, "Wait a minute, Mary." She put the phone down, and I heard her telling a misbehaving four-year-old great-great-grandson, "Sit your ass on that chair now." He sat.

B told me her birthday was April 9 when I asked. She said her birth certificate says she was born on April 6, but there's no doubt in B's mind when she was born. "My mother said I was born on April 9, and I guess she's the one that would know!" I agree. April 9.

Beatrice loved flowers and loved to work in her yard but didn't have time when she was caring for Mother. So for her birthday, which she just considered another day, my brother and I hired a gardener to dig a flower bed on the side of B's house. She lived on the corner of a small cul-de-sac, so she could see the side and back door of her mustard-colored brick house each day when she drove home from Mom's. She would drive in the driveway, park by that side of her house, and walk up to the short, covered walkway that led from the garage into her kitchen. All the while, she would see her new flowers.

The small flower bed was put in with some spring flowers while she was at work. That may be the best birthday gift I'll ever give to anyone. B was so happy and proud of her new flowers. An undemonstrative person became demonstrative.

When friends would comment on her flower bed, she told me what she said to them, and it touched me deeply. B said, "I tell people if I ever had a friend, it's Mary, my friend Mary. She's the same every day, never changes from one day to the next." I will never receive a compliment that means more to me than I did from this grounded, wise, and content woman.

16

The Legacy of the Blue Chair

Once B became sick in her 80s and needed help, Vera took care of her for a while. Then she lived with her daughter and son-in-law, Marvella and Tennell Atkins. Her home on Gillette sold, the home she had loved and the home that had welcomed so many.

Marvella said one day when I called that her mother was doing better, and I could tell when I said "Hi, B" to her on the phone. For 20 years, every time I called B, I always began with "Hi, B. It's Mary," and I'd hear the "B laugh." The laugh was gone, but she was still Beatrice.

A helper came a few times each week to help B dress, shower, and give much-needed relief to Marvella. Later it became necessary for daily help. Beatrice accepted where she was in life. She was now the patient and not the caregiver.

This change in Beatrice's health was, at first, a difficult adjustment for her big family. Their matriarch, the firecracker who always cooked family dinners, gave instructions like bullets flying, gave a bed if needed, and answered any problem had a body wearing out, and at times, a mind that got mixed up. No one will ever take the place of Beatrice Jones: mother, grandmother, great-grandmother, great-great-grandmother, nurse, friend, cook, counselor, giver, example, and even patient.

B fought diabetes, high blood pressure, and heart disease her entire adult life, and those problems never went away. I learned this over time, after she began helping Mom, because B never let those diseases affect her work and life, if possible. Now she kept her spunk on good days. On other days, she slept a lot, probably catching up on sleep missed from decades of hard work, heartache, and loving others. The small strokes started and dementia was more frequent. Marvella cared for her mother as her mother cared for her children and so many sick people. If ever anyone deserved to be cared for, it was Beatrice.

Even ten years after my mother's death, there was a tangible tie that still connected Beatrice and my mother. The blue chair. The infamous blue chair. The blue chair that caused such an uproar the day it arrived for my mother. The blue chair my mother angrily told the delivery men to take away. The blue chair Beatrice insisted they keep. The blue chair where my mother sat, read, napped, ate chocolate she'd hidden in the side pocket, and rested in until the day before she died. The blue chair where Mom, B, and I talked so many times.

The blue chair was passed down from my mother to Beatrice. The blue chair was where Beatrice, in her 80s, sat, ate, and watched TV, as others cared for her. The blue chair was where Beatrice sat when I would go see her. The blue chair was now hers. The blue chair that represents the story of an incredibly deep and beautiful and unique friendship.

Part II: Beatrice

17

The "Athens of Texas"

Beatrice Dilworth Jones was born April 9, 1930, in Clarksville. Exactly one month later, in Sherman, Texas, 90 miles due west of Clarksville, an event occurred that would haunt race relations in Northeast Texas during the early years of Beatrice's life.

May 9, 1930, was a day of murder and terror in Sherman, Texas, and a day that destroyed the reputation of this booming Texas town and struck fear in the lives of black people. The Sherman Riot of 1930 was one of the most gruesome acts of racial violence in Texas history. Scars still exist. Books like *Texas Ranger* by John Boessenecker, *1012 Natchez* by Dr. Njoki McElroy, and articles from *The Texas Handbook Online* by the Texas State Historical Association reported details of what happened that terrifying day and night.

Sherman was proud of being called the "Athens of Texas" because of its phenomenal growth and prosperity in the early part of the 20th century. With a population of 16,000, the town had a booming cotton industry, a railway system, four colleges, beautiful parks and churches, a stately 19th-century stone courthouse, and Chamber of Commerce boasting of "law and order." Sherman, Texas, was bustling and growing.

Although Jim Crow laws ruled in the South, the segregated black community of 2,000 in Sherman prospered with a vibrant business community, drug store, dental office, movie theater, fraternal lodges, and a well-to-do residential area. This thriving black community, developed by motivated entrepreneurs, was centered on Mulberry Street, four blocks north of the stately courthouse. Within 24 hours, on May 9, 1930, this prosperous black business community was in ashes, and the vibrancy and pride in the "Athens of Texas" was obliterated overnight.

Earlier that week, a white woman had accused George Hughes, a black man, of rape. The woman lived with her husband and small son on a farm outside of the town. Hughes was arrested and confessed.

He was arrested on a Monday, and the trial was set for Friday. The intensity of outrage from white townspeople was the reason a worried judge set the trial as soon as possible. In this town, the case would have been open and shut to a jury, but now angry whites were demanding justice—their justice. A black man guilty of raping a white woman should suffer and die. The incensed whites would be the executioners.

By early morning on May 9, the day of the trial, the number of enraged whites had multiplied into hundreds of townspeople and farmers. They had not succeeded in getting the prisoner for themselves earlier, but now with increased numbers, this angry mob became more demanding and raucous as they marched to the courthouse for the 9:30 trial of George Hughes.

The Texas governor, aware of this tense situation in

Sherman, had ordered four Texas Rangers to guard the prisoner from the irate mob as he was escorted to the courthouse. A large crowd packed the courthouse downstairs, in the halls upstairs and down, up the two winding staircases, and outside the closed courtroom on the second floor. Around 11:00 that morning, just as the jury had been picked, the judge abruptly stopped proceedings because of disruption from the infuriated mob inside the courthouse and outside on the grounds and street. The Rangers were able to clear the courthouse.

By 12:00 noon, the enraged mob had increased from hundreds to several thousand townspeople, farmers, and spectators. The mob stormed the courthouse four times, each time repelled by the Rangers, and each time more brazen. The men in the mob put women in front to protect themselves from the Rangers inside. Because of the women, Rangers were told to use their guns only as clubs to beat the crowd back and not to shoot.

Twice the crowd was repelled. The third time, two Rangers made a decision to use their guns to keep from being overwhelmed by the wild mob. They fired warning shots and threw tear gas to break up the crowd, forcing the men and women back into the street. Immediately the Rangers ran to the courtroom, grabbed George Hughes, and rushed him to the safety of an impenetrable steel and concrete cell on the second floor.

Law enforcement was ineffective and outnumbered by the raging mob, now nearly 5,000. By early afternoon, many of these men were armed with rocks, axes, and dynamite. Breaking glass sounded as rocks were hurled at courthouse windows. The sound fed the blood-thirsty mob even more. Axes splintered the wood of the beautiful courthouse doors. As the doors broke open, a large crowd pushed into the courthouse, filling the stairways and courtroom in a frenzied search for their victim. Unable to find Hughes, the angry crowd spilled back onto the street.

Around 2:30 p.m., gasoline was thrown on the outside of the courthouse, and the elegant, 19th-century stone edifice, once sitting proudly in the center of a peaceful town square, was engulfed in flames that quickly shot skyward. Firehoses were sliced. Firemen were helpless as they watched their courthouse be destroyed by raging flames caused by citizens of their own town.

By 4:00 p.m., the incendiary mob had celebrated their historic courthouse burn to the ground with only the steel and concrete vault holding George Hughes left standing. The four Rangers tried valiantly to fight their way to the vault to get the prisoner to safety, but the raging flames made it impossible. In less than two hours, the stately courthouse that had been the beacon of justice in the "Athens of Texas" was razed to the ground by this out-of-control mob.

At 6:00 p.m., a large contingent of Texas National Guardsmen arrived, and the still crazed mob fought them off with rocks, boards, and soda bottles. National Guardsmen were forced to retreat with "missiles arching at their heads and the mob howling at their heels." It was impossible for four Texas Rangers, the too small contingent of National Guardsmen, and the sheriff with his men to control this bloodthirsty mob. The civilized town of Sherman, once heralded as the "law and order" town, was gone.

Dark descended, and a spotlight had been placed to shine on the vault where George Hughes had been rushed earlier in the day. A small group of obsessed lynchers climbed a ladder to the vault to get to the despised Hughes. Once at the top, they used acetylene torches and dynamite to finally break through the steel and concrete. Sherman police were directing traffic while these men were blowing open the vault. One of the crazed men finally bellowed victoriously, "Here he is!"

Raucous cheers erupted from the deranged mob below as they broke into an exuberant rendition of "Happy Days Are Here Again." Now their justice would finally have its turn, but the prisoner was already dead. He had died earlier that afternoon from smoke inhalation from the fire. The mob didn't care; dead or alive, George Hughes's body was now their property.

According to eyewitness accounts, the prisoner's body was yanked out of the vault, his legs and arms splayed grotesquely. His body was dragged to the ladder and "dropped down the ladder, striking the ground with a thud." The body was then chained and dragged slowly, four blocks north of the destroyed courthouse to Mulberry Street where the vibrant business center of Sherman's black community was located. The mob, although thinning, never stopped yelling encouragement to their leaders.

By midnight, the cheering mob, still including women and babies, had diminished to 2,000 who watched with glee as the bloodied, broken body of George Hughes was hanged from a tree.

Looters broke glass fronts of the thriving black businesses—throwing furniture out to use as kindling under the body of the prisoner. A sharp knife appeared and was used to cut off the parts of George Hughes's body that had made him male. These parts were then passed around the crowd on a piece of newspaper.

Matches were struck. The furniture used for kindling quickly became a bonfire. What had been a living, breathing man, 12 hours before, was now hanging from a tree and barely visible in the blazing flames that erupted beneath him. George Hughes's broken body roasted over the roaring fire while parts of the mob kept singing, looting, and burning black businesses. The remaining mob celebrated by smoking cigarettes and eating candy from the black drugstore.

Firemen were attacked and prevented from doing anything to stop the raging fires. A hotel, doctor's office, dentist's office, barber shop, restaurant, movie theater, and drug store were destroyed. "The hopes and dreams of black entrepreneurs and professionals lay strewn about in the soggy ashes, rubble, and ruin," stated Dr. McElroy in *1012 Natchez*, and "the black neighborhood was never rebuilt," reported John Boessenecker in *Texas Ranger*.

In the early hours of the next morning, Saturday, May 10, detachments of National Guard from Dallas and Fort Worth, ordered by the governor, arrived and began their military march to the black neighborhood. The National Guard and drizzle that had turned to heavy rain cleared the streets of the spent mob by dawn. The Sherman riot was over.

Mercifully, one of the soldiers cut down Hughes's mutilated, charred body from the cottonwood tree where it hung. George Hughes was buried in an unmarked grave in the black cemetery outside of Sherman.

The heinous events that had occurred were reported in *The New York Times* and national newspapers the next day. Sherman and the riot and lynching quickly became international news. The Texas governor declared martial law and increased the number of National Guardsmen in a town that two days before had been heralded as the "Athens of Texas." Martial law in Sherman, ninety miles from Clarksville, lasted two weeks, but the impact and the scars from that horrific 24-hour period remain today. Boessenecker wrote these chilling words: "History—the unforgiving mistress of truth—will not allow us to forget that civilization, like George Hughes, perished for one hellish day on the funeral pyre in Sherman."

The Sherman lynching incited more violence and lynchings in Northeast Texas where Beatrice, seven brothers and sisters, and their hard-working parents lived. Shortly after Sherman, lynching of another black man occurred in Honey Grove, even closer to Clarksville and the Dilworths. More lynchings followed in Gainesville, Paris, and Dallas. This was the volatile racial environment in which Beatrice grew up.

On May 9, 1930, Beatrice was exactly one month old. Ophelia might have been rocking Beatrice as the angry mob threw bricks and rocks at the windows of the Sherman County Courthouse. She might have been nursing Baby Beatrice as gasoline was thrown on the courthouse and fire consumed the stately building that had represented truth and justice. Ophelia might have been crooning to her infant as the accused black man's body was dragged from his cell, mutilated, and burned. Whatever Ophelia was doing, life changed in Northeast Texas that day.

18

Growing Up in
Jim Crow Texas

Ophelia and Searcey Dilworth, Beatrice's parents, lived
in the black section of Clarksville known as Haywood.
They worked hard to make ends meet. Searcey farmed cotton
and corn, working as a sharecropper, although he did own
a small piece of land. According to Todd Atkins, Beatrice's
grandson, his grandfather worked from "sunup to sundown."
Ophelia took care of their eight children and saw her family
was well-fed and clothed with clean, ironed clothes. She often
took jobs caring for the sick, working at the black school, or
babysitting and cleaning for white folks in town.

Life was hard, but families and neighbors in Haywood created a tight-knit community. Christian values of love, respect,
and hard work were taught to the children by example, words,
and discipline.

Beatrice's great-great-grandfather had been a slave on the

Dilworth plantation in Mississippi. When the Civil War ended and Abraham Lincoln signed the Emancipation Proclamation, B's great-great-grandfather was no longer someone's property. This former slave was given the surname of his previous owner and became Mr. Dilworth. Every slave owner had been required to give each freed slave one hundred acres of land, and the acreage bequeathed to Beatrice's great-great-grandfather was in Clarksville, Texas, a town that had been founded only thirty years before.

Lack of literacy and money kept freed slaves beholden to sharecroppers. Sharecropping kept blacks from an education and substantial income even three generations after slavery ended. Through the years, the one hundred acres given to Beatrice's great-great-grandfather had been split among multiple children and grandchildren. Beatrice's father, Searcey Dilworth, still rented from a sharecropper even in 1930. This was 65 years after the end of the Civil War. B's beloved father could not read or write. Searcey Dilworth signed his name with an "X."

Segregation was the accepted way of life in Texas during Beatrice Jones's childhood and young adulthood. Segregation existed in almost all public places and facilities. These included restrooms, water fountains, schools and colleges, restaurants, movie theaters, libraries, barber shops, train stations, trains, and buses. There were white residential areas and designated black residential areas. The Emancipation Proclamation changed life on paper but not socially, politically, or economically for the black race in Texas and the South.

Education remained a blatant, impacting aspect of racism for African Americans. Still substandard. Still inferior educational facilities, funding, curriculums, books, and inadequate salaries for teachers. Attendance was often cut short in rural areas because the children were needed to help on farms. This kept black children from gaining the education that could provide future and better job opportunities and from affecting social change.

Beatrice's brothers attended school but were taken out to pick cotton when it was in season. Putting the children to work in the cotton fields brought in money enough to feed the family and pay taxes while, at the same time, compromising a significant part of their education. Beatrice's mother did not complain that her children lacked the schooling white children had. Instead, Beatrice described how her mother saw that her children always had clean clothes and got to school, all the while emphasizing the importance of an education for each.

Work opportunities and pay were meager for blacks. Common jobs were yard work, sharecropping, or being a maid or cook. Beatrice's family performed their jobs, whatever they were, with pride. These practices continued until the 1960s, a century after the Emancipation Proclamation. Beatrice's parents followed the path prescribed for blacks in the South on their small farm in Clarksville, Texas.

Dr. Njoki McElroy, a professor at SMU, is the age of Beatrice. She is a black woman who grew up in Dallas and Sherman. She and Beatrice likely would have been good friends and shared stories and laughter had their paths crossed.

Dr. McElroy clarified first-hand the deference demanded from blacks as she and Beatrice grew up: "You said, 'Yes sir, no sir'. . . . You didn't talk loud. You dressed a certain way. It served a dual purpose—to represent your people and white people. . . . There was colored, there was white. You got used to your reality. You got it; whites had a sense of superiority, blacks a sense of inferiority. The black community was so encompassing though. They were your people. You felt warm and cared for within the black community. It protected you and guarded you. Other black families, too, kept you from reacting in a negative way toward injustice."

The story of growing up in "pre-civil rights Dallas, a time of rigid segregation and Jim Crow laws," was recorded in Dr. McElroy's memoir, *1012 Natchez*. She remembered, as a five-year-old, the "urgent bulletin" on the radio in her Dallas home telling news of the Sherman Riot. She remembered the panic her mother felt because her mother's parents, Dr. McElroy's grandparents, lived in Sherman, 60 miles from Dallas, and were in imminent danger.

Dr. McElroy's grandparents were an important part of the vibrant black community in Sherman. The urgent radio bulletin had said, "It was rumored that if the mob could not get to Hughes, they were going to go after every Negro in Sherman and burn their houses down."

This riot was almost 90 years ago, yet the memories are still vivid in Dr. McElroy's mind. For her, at age five, the hate and reality of the deep chasm between blacks and whites became real that day—May 9, 1930, just as they had for Beatrice's family in Clarksville.

Dr. McElroy told me how it felt to be treated as inferior. Had Beatrice felt this way? Had her parents? When I asked Beatrice about racism when she was young, her answer was brief. I was hopeful for a glimmer of emotion and memory about difficult years of segregation, at least some resentment of the injustices perpetrated on herself, her children, and her race. My question to her was from friend to friend.

I shouldn't have been surprised that B showed little concern with segregation growing up. She was young, and her family, school, community, and church were her life at that time.

As she got older, white people gave her work and income. Beatrice Dilworth Jones refused to allow resentment to affect her attitude. Her job was to raise educated, Christian children, support her family, live her faith, and deal with social issues within herself and her own family. Those priorities were a full-time job.

As a young adult and mother in Dallas, of course, Beatrice was aware of the racial turmoil that affected her race and her children. When her children had difficult days at school because of integration and white resentment, Beatrice saw her job not as marching down to the school and complaining but as teaching her children how to deal with difficult situations in life.

The irony is that while white superiority and subjugation of blacks did exist culturally, socially, and economically in Clarksville, African Americans had their own tight-knit families, culture, and support within Haywood, their assigned black community. Ophelia and Searcey had their people where warmth and care existed; surrounded by loving parents, brothers and sisters, a warm community, and church, Beatrice was secure.

Twenty counties, out of 254 Texas counties, from Red River County down to Houston, experienced some form of terror from the Ku Klux Klan, the secret society that vehemently opposed any mixing of whites and blacks. The Klan resorted to intimidation and violence while hiding behind white masks and robes. Members of the Klan were from every segment of society and even included town leaders, politicians, and law enforcement officials.

In the early 1920s, Texas Klan membership numbered in tens of thousands. They were private but public. Private since they hid their identity behind white hoods, public because these groups would parade through towns and conduct cross-burnings. The single purpose was to intimidate and show white power. Most of the Klan's activities were in Northeast Texas. Clarksville, county seat of Red River County and home of Beatrice's family, was in the hub of Klan activity.

Then May 9, 1930, happened. The Sherman Riot was one of the worst incidents of racial violence in the nation at the beginning of the Great Depression. The anger, the rioting, and the lynching were so terrifying that many black citizens of Sherman fled their homes or farms and hid in brush or sewers until the National Guard arrived and took control. Sherman was the county seat and had been a town of industry, education, and banking. Now it was infamous for one of the most barbaric acts man could inflict on a fellow human being.

The proud, black businesses of Sherman were gone in one day. A mob had destroyed the difficult work and hard-fought success of professionals and entrepreneurs who had built a good and respectable life in this North Texas town.

The Sherman Riot and subsequent increases of violence collided with a bleak economic situation across the country. Black families were not only dealing with the reality of violent racism but also grueling hours farming and desperate poverty with the onset of the Depression.

Beatrice Dilworth Jones lived through decades of poverty, intolerance, and change. What did not change was the strength and fortitude of that little girl on a farm in Clarksville, the bold young woman who moved to Amarillo to study nursing, and the wife and mother who braved difficulties and heartache in her life.

19

Breaking the Color Barrier

Almost two decades after the Sherman Riot, soldiers were home from the war, and the American social and cultural scene began to change. During World War II, many, including Negroes, moved from farm to city to work in defense factories that were aiding in the war effort. Rules of segregation had eased, ever so slightly, when President Roosevelt allowed blacks to work in these factories. Whites and African Americans saw opportunities in the city they had not had before on a farm, and many stayed. Demographics changed with Negroes in closer touch with each other in the city.

When black soldiers returned from fighting, rumblings of anger and demands for change began. These black soldiers saw the irony of fighting for freedom and rights that they were not granted in their own country. They'd fought against Nazi racism but not Jim Crow racism.

World War II marked a major shift in bringing the injustices of segregation out into the open, culminating in the passage of the Civil Rights Act in 1964. This legislation was certainly a big step but did not solve the myriad of problems plaguing racism. The years after the war up to 1964 and even years after that were angry and often violent times between blacks and whites, especially in the South.

Two young African Americans who took advantage of opportunities offered them after the war lived and worked through these tumultuous years of shifting race relations in the country. One experienced this upheaval on a national stage, the other on a smaller stage of family, work, and community. Jackie Robinson and Beatrice Jones are examples of individuals in public and private spheres who, as adults, exhibited grit and determination when confronting seemingly never-ending and impossible odds of racial injustice.

Jackie Robinson was the first black baseball player to break the color barrier in Major League Baseball (MLB) in the 20th century. On April 15, 1947, he took the field as a Brooklyn Dodger amid heckling and jeers. Robinson played for the Dodgers for ten years and won Rookie of the Year his first year by leading the National League in stolen bases.

Jackie was born on a Georgia sharecropper's farm in 1919, grandson of a slave. One year later, his father abandoned the family, and his mother moved the family to California where she worked as a maid to support her children. Jackie's mother broke her own color barrier by the Robinsons being the first Negro family to live in their Pasadena neighborhood. She also had a deep faith that was instilled in her young son. As a child, Jackie experienced racial abuse when, constantly, rocks were thrown and racial slurs yelled at his home. By the age of eight, he fought back. This was Jackie Robinson's first battle with civil rights.

As an adolescent, he became part of a gang but was saved

from juvenile delinquency by a neighbor who became his first father figure. This man's influence and his brother's guidance encouraged Jackie toward sports where he could direct his anger and energy.

Junior college seemed promising, yet hostility surfaced once again. Jackie's football teammates, mostly from the South, strenuously objected to a black player on the team, but he held the trump card. He knew he was the team's best player and said he would quit if the dissension continued. Players wanted to win more than be segregated, so Robinson was accepted by his teammates. He reciprocated by accepting those who had been against him, and these young men jelled as a team, soon having an undefeated season with Jackie as the star. He was an outstanding all-around athlete, continuing to win numerous awards and honors.

This young African American gained confidence from his successes but, as in childhood, began openly fighting back against racial slurs, even with policemen. Once again, a father figure stepped in his life at just the right time. This man was pastor of a nearby Methodist church and able to guide Jackie toward a spiritual life to help deal with his anger. From time spent with this mentor, Jackie's faith grew, and he even taught Sunday School. There were no more skirmishes with the police.

At University of California, Los Angeles (UCLA), Robinson was the first player ever to letter in all four sports. Football, track, basketball, and baseball continued to give him a venue in which to direct his anger and then his grief over the death of his big brother who had been his greatest fan. At UCLA, Jackie fell in love with his future wife. In addition to his mother and pastor, Rachel was also a woman of deep faith, and after marriage, she was always a rock for her husband, especially in the tortuous years when he was the first black player in the 20th century playing baseball on a National League team.

When America entered World War II, Robinson joined the army. After enduring bigotry in childhood and college, an incident occurred where he once again stood against injustice. He'd already been blackballed by his commanding officers who refused to let a black man play on the army baseball team. Robinson's physical outlet for dealing with injustice was gone.

One day while stationed in Ft. Hood, Jackie boarded a military bus and was ordered to go to the back of the bus. He refused and was court-martialed. This charge ended Robinson's military career even though the charges for the court-martial were dismissed, and he was honorably discharged. He ended up in Kansas City playing baseball with a Negro baseball league, and there, Jackie Robinson's life changed forever.

The Brooklyn Dodgers and its president, Branch Rickey, had been considering the unprecedented move of integrating their team to end the "gentlemen's agreement" that prevented major league owners from signing African American players to their rosters. But—they needed a player who could do more than play baseball. Rickey knew any black player they drafted would be a target of racial abuse and thought Jackie Robinson could handle the abuse without hurting the team and hurting the racial step forward he hoped to make. Talmage Boston in his book, *Baseball and the Baby Boomer,* referred to Rickey's brave and unconventional move as the "Noble Experiment."

Robinson's baseball skills, character, and "conservative, family-oriented lifestyle" drew the interest of the Dodger president. Boston described other character facets that qualified him for this experiment. Jackie's mother, his pastor, and Rachel were close to him and strong, moral individuals he never wanted to disappoint. Jackie was college educated, "spoke well, and was battle-tested in interracial athletic competition." He controlled his temper.

Baseball and the Baby Boomer describes the well-known meeting that took place between Jackie and the Dodger president who was called the "'ferocious gentleman.'" For several hours, Rickey repeatedly hurled taunts and insults at Robinson because he had to know how his potential black player, one whose addition would cause a national uproar, would respond to the ugliness that would occur. The manager needed a player "with the guts not to fight back." Robinson passed the test and was signed to a Dodgers contract. Jackie Robinson was now the trailblazer for Negroes to play professional sports.

On April 15, 1947, he took the field as first baseman with the Brooklyn Dodgers and broke the color barrier in MLB for the first time in the 20th century. Two years later, he had the highest batting average and was named the league's Most Valuable Player (MVP). His outstanding play helped lead the Dodgers to six National League championships and one World Series victory. His baserunning has been described as unnerving opponents' pitchers and terrorizing infielders trying to keep him from stealing bases.

Although Robinson's baseball career was extraordinary, his personal life during these tumultuous years was agonizing. The racial abuses he endured included some of his own Dodger teammates protesting against playing with a Negro, opponents intentionally pitching at his head, and runners deliberately sliding into base so they could spike him with their shoes. There were unrelenting taunts, jeers, thrown bottles from fans, and death threats to him, his wife, and his children. Jim Crow laws prohibited him from staying in hotels and eating in restaurants with his team. Robinson's loving wife and children stood by him through these dark days. Jackie Robinson just kept playing baseball and doing his job.

Robinson once said, "Plenty of times I wanted to haul off when somebody insulted me for the color of my skin, but I had to hold to myself. I knew I was kind of an experiment. The whole thing was bigger than me." Focus and dignity were the quiet weapons Robinson chose to fight with against the interminable racial abuse. His courageous and nonviolent fight, together with incredible baseball skill, served to make him the true champion he became. Jackie Robinson fought daily for his black race to have the same rights as people with white skin long before the Civil Rights Act and long before the United States Army was integrated.

Two important individuals supported Robinson as well as the integration of baseball. One was the commissioner, and one was Robinson's teammate. When the St. Louis Cardinals threatened to strike if Robinson played in their game, the commissioner of baseball retorted that any player who did this would be suspended from baseball. The game was played.

In another Dodgers game, the incessant taunting became so bad that one of the Dodger team captains left his position on the field, walked to where Robinson was playing, and put his arm around the derided Jackie Robinson. This simple gesture of loyalty and support to his teammate spoke volumes to players, coaches, and fans. The player, Pee Wee Reese, and Robinson remained close friends the rest of their lives.

Although Robinson retired from his legendary baseball career after ten years, he continued his commitment to fight for the rights of African Americans in a free country where our Declaration of Independence states "all men are created equal" but where blacks had never been equal. His activism began when he was eight years old and continued in high school and college, at Ft. Hood, in MLB, and until his death.

After retiring from baseball, Robinson began speaking for the National Association for the Advancement of Colored People (NAACP) and appeared several times with Martin Luther King, Jr. In 1962, six years after retirement from baseball and his first year of eligibility, Robinson was inducted as the first black player into the Baseball Hall of Fame in Cooperstown, New York. His autobiography was published in 1972, the year he died. On his tombstone are his words: "A life is not important except in the impact it has on others." The Presidential Medal of Freedom, the highest honor an American citizen can receive, was awarded to Jackie Robinson, twelve years after his death, in 1984. Jackie Robinson impacted adults and children of all colors and ages all across America. He is still remembered and honored today, especially on Jackie Robinson Day, April 15, the day he first took the field in 1947.

On the 50th anniversary of Jackie Robinson's breaking the color barrier in baseball, his uniform #42 was retired from the Brooklyn Dodgers and all MLB teams as a tribute to the courage, skill, and impact this brave man had on baseball and American civil rights.

Since 2009, only on April 15, all MLB players and on-field personnel wear Jackie's number, #42, to remember Robinson's significance to baseball and our country. George Will called Jackie's signing and playing with the Dodgers "'the opening salvo in the American Civil Rights Movement.'"

Jackie Robinson's life serves as a backdrop on a national

stage for Beatrice Jones's life on a more private stage. The entire country and thousands upon thousands of fans observed this brave young man on the baseball field while a community of family, neighbors, friends, church members, patients, patients' families, and an untold number of strangers observed this brave woman on a day-to-day basis. Jackie's fight for equality for blacks affected Beatrice indirectly. He paved the way for blacks in professional sports, therefore paving the way for future change in many areas where segregation existed.

Although ten years younger than Jackie Robinson, Beatrice was born on a sharecropper's farm in the Jim Crow South just as he was, yet she grew up on that same farm in Northeast Texas unlike Jackie who grew up in urban California. Both individuals were raised in relative obscurity until adulthood when Robinson became a public figure. In their Jim Crow days of growing up, Beatrice and Robinson had different experiences in different parts of the country.

When Beatrice was young, all she knew were black schools. There were no organized team sports. The children in the family spent hours and hours in the hot sun picking cotton. Beatrice was with her large family daily, which included both parents who had a great influence on her. Church was all-important to her parents, and they saw the family attended church every Sunday and sometimes during the week. Beatrice's strong faith began to develop in her childhood and grew to be the foundation on which she lived her life. Beatrice and her family had a strong and supportive black community where she lived in Clarksville.

The undercurrent of racial tensions became undeniable after the war, which was the time Beatrice left home for nursing school. After getting her LVN, she worked, married, moved to Dallas, and had babies. She and N.D. lived in one of the mandated black neighborhoods, Oak Cliff.

The growing intensity of black activism quickly created a volatile society at the time Beatrice and N.D. were raising a family. On May 17, 1954, the Supreme Court of the United States made a unanimous, milestone decision in the case of *Brown v. Board of Education*. Supreme Court Justice Earl Warren delivered the ruling: "State-sanctioned segregation of public schools was a violation of the 14th Amendment and was therefore unconstitutional." This paved the way for the Civil Rights Act of 1964 that ended segregation in public places and banned discrimination by employers on the basis of "race, color, religion, sex, or national origin."

These two pieces of legislation were historic and opened wide the doors for blacks to enter society as equals. However, rulings by the Supreme Court and laws passed by Congress that mandated equality could not guarantee equality. The United States government had changed the laws but gave no direction for how to implement these laws.

Rioting and often violence continued for years. These were turbulent times, but because of activism and legislation, the age-old tradition of segregation was slowly but surely being uprooted. Desegregation took years in the Dallas schools, and it took decades for civil rights to be accepted in Texas. That is still a work in progress.

The 1950s, 1960s, and 1970s, years of escalating violence and race riots, were the years Beatrice and her husband were working and raising children. All five of the children experienced taunting and at times physical abuse from fellow white students. Their children reacted in different ways, but the abuse had an impact on each. Marvella told the story of having milk cartons thrown at her and her younger brother in the high school cafeteria by white athletes with no correction or disciplinary measures given to the offenders.

Instead of fighting their battles for them, Beatrice taught her children the way she believed in fighting and that involved a strong sense of self-respect. Her way mirrored Jackie Robinson's way: "You know who you are. Hold your head high. Keep movin' forward." Beatrice was working two jobs and had neither time nor the inclination to interfere.

At times when Beatrice was with her children in public, there were taunts and insults she endured or addressed. She considered people who would call her and her children "niggers" ignorant—people not worthy of her attention. "Keep movin' forward" or "just walk on by" was the way Beatrice Jones fought derogatory treatment almost all the time. Almost all.

There were infrequent occasions when Beatrice did take a stand against inequality, and her children remember these times vividly. Marvella told a memorable story of her mother's quiet strength in the face of injustice. "We were in Clarksville at a barbecue place where blacks would pay in front and had to pick their food up in the back."

Beatrice refused to go to the back, and with her children huddled around her, she respectfully told the cashier, "If you take my money here, you can give me my food here." They refused.

"Mama turned to us kids and said, 'We're not gonna eat here. Nope. We're not staying.' We begged, 'Please, please Mama, we want that barbecue so bad!! Please! We're not stayin' to eat?' Mama wouldn't let us stay." Beatrice quietly left with her children tagging behind.

How did Beatrice know when to take a stand and when to "walk on by?" Because of her own self-worth and self-respect, as well as her children's self-worth and self-respect, she knew when these times were. She and her children were just as good as the whites at the front, and her children needed to know that. Beatrice took a stand. That lesson was more important than feeding hungry children at that moment.

Marvella gave more insight: "I think Mama learned from Ophelia, her mama. In Clarksville, the message to blacks had been to 'stay in your place.' Her mother would say, 'When they treat you that way, just make sure you're nice and clean and have your manners.' When the white people in town got to know Ophelia and Searcey, they respected them." Beatrice saw an example of dignity and confidence from her parents.

Beatrice Jones and Jackie Robinson handled insults the same way—with dignity and nonviolence. Neither backed down nor did they react negatively. Beatrice focused on what was her priority—working and raising her five children. Jackie played baseball and was a father and husband.

B's life, her example and actions, taught her children how to conduct themselves. Her nonreactive but direct and confident actions spoke volumes. Leaving the barbeque shack echoed Jackie's refusal to go to the back of the bus in Ft. Hood. Beatrice did not yell, nor was she violent. She remained composed, confident, and respectful. Just as Jackie Robinson, she knew her worth was not in her skin color and didn't have to prove it.

Beatrice's work was quiet; Robinson's was not. Their environments and careers differed, yet each honed individual skills amid great difficulties and injustices. Their impact on others was huge. They elevated themselves to what Boston, in *Baseball and the Baby Boomer*, referred to as "that higher level of emotional intelligence." That and the spiritual foundation of each gave strength for nonreactive responses to cruel taunts and impacted those in the sphere of their influence. Robinson broke the color barrier in professional baseball in front of masses of people. Beatrice broke color barriers, privately, with the patients and patients' families for whom she worked.

20

"Keep on Livin'"

Memories connect the threads of the life of an individual, the life of a family, and the lives of generations. Some of the impactful and major events of Beatrice Jones's life as well as daily occurrences and stories fill the memories of family members and families for whom Beatrice worked. At times, memories of the same event are seen differently. One thing that never differed was the love, respect, and impact Beatrice made on her family and those who had been privileged to be part of her life.

Beatrice's focus was grounded in her faith, and her life reflected that. She never had to prove her self-worth—she knew it as a Christian. That was the guiding light of her daily walk whatever the circumstance. Her compassion, love for others, gratitude, and wisdom are reflected in her daughters' memories. Beatrice was a behind-the-scenes hero—not one the world might acknowledge but one who made the world a better place in which to live.

Beatrice used to laugh talking about Vera fighting down the street when she was young. She said, "When she was growing up, I'd drive by and see Vera beatin' up boys down the street bigger than she was because they'd tease Marvella." Beatrice didn't interfere with her kids and neighborhood kids. She didn't panic, get upset, or get out of the car to fix things. She let her children work out their own problems.

Vera confirmed her mother's story. "I was a fighter. Don and I were the fighters. I'd fight the boys or anybody. You couldn't say anything about my brothers or sisters. It was usually Marvella. She would cry if you said 'boo.' So she was teased a lot."

Beatrice was a fighter, too, but not physically. Even as a child, she shied away from fighting. Her daddy once threatened to "whip her" if she didn't take up for herself. B found her own way of fighting when things weren't fair. She ignored demeaning comments and went on with her day, work, or life. The number of times B said "just let it go" to her children for real or perceived wrongs are too numerous to count. Rude people were not worth spending time worrying about. She might have said to her children, "Just let it go. Your job is to get your homework done and set the table, not worry about what they said. Go do your homework."

Beatrice was clear on her Christian values of family, work, respect, and love, and she refused to fight battles that didn't matter. Her usual philosophy of countering unjust treatment was "why pay attention to ignorant people?" Ignorant people were troublemakers: those who called others derogatory names, those who would pick a fight, or those determined to stir up trouble. She didn't have to prove others wrong. Beatrice knew who she was.

B ignored a lot of bad behavior, but there were a few times

she chose not to ignore—times she deemed important enough to take a stand. Another example of this was when her children were with her and a rude person would comment on the light skin color of Curtis, Don, or Marvella. She didn't fight, yell, or threaten. Instead Beatrice had her own clever way of responding with confidence, self-respect, and clarity, and these quiet stands made an impact on her children and others. Beatrice was an example of calm in dealing with life when life was not fair whether she ignored and kept on moving or whether she responded.

B and N.D. were attentive parents. N.D., especially, was protective of his girls. Vera remembered her daddy when she was small. "Daddy was not strict except with the girls. If we were watching TV and our panties were showing, he'd say, 'Put your dress down.' If we were outside playing and our dress flew up, he'd say 'Your dress is too short. I can see your panties.' He did not like that." Raising five children wasn't easy. B and N.D. were in their 30s, and times were hard and money scarce, but no matter. Their children would learn proper manners.

Vera described her mother as "a hard worker and very loving. She loved her kids. She would do anything for anybody— go the extra mile for anybody. She was very funny. Mama was the laughter of the whole family. She'd make everybody joyful." That was the consensus of B's children.

As the children grew, B had to go back to work to make ends meet. "My mama worked in a nursing home on Corinth Street that Daddy helped build." N.D. worked construction. Vera was proud of her parents and liked the connection of both to this nursing home.

"Then Mama worked at Parkland and St. Paul's. She worked in the ER, labor and delivery, and the nursery at Parkland and at St. Paul's on the floor as an LVN." Vera remembers taking her mother to these jobs. Each of the children—Curtis, Vera, Don, Marvella, and Rickey—learned what hard work was by watching their parents, and with two parents working, they began to pitch in and help at home.

As her children got older, there were more serious situations at school with the federal enforcement of integration. B was a working mother, and when there were problems at school, she told her children, "You know who you are. Hold your head up. Keep a movin'." Beatrice was not a helicopter parent.

School and education stayed at the forefront of priorities for the Jones's children, including after-school activities. Vera loved eighth grade, but more than academics, she wanted to be on the drill squad because she loved to dance. With her mother and daddy working, she was afraid they couldn't afford to get her uniform. "The uniforms were very expensive, around $300, and that was a lot of money. I had to talk to my parents about the uniform."

"Mama, I wanna dance on the drill squad so bad. I wanna dance with them. You and Daddy would have to buy my uniform though."

"No, honey, we just don't have the money." B was matter-of-fact.

Vera approached her father. "I'll give it to you, Vera. Don't worry about it. I'll get it."

"I got the uniform. My last year in high school, I was the one to go out on the field and blow the whistle for everyone to come out on the field. I went to Roosevelt. The uniforms were sky blue and white."

Vera remembered the respect and cooperation between her two parents. "Mama was fine with Daddy getting me the uniform. It made Mama happy. She wanted me to have it anyway." Vera loved and respected her parents as did her four siblings.

After N.D. died from cancer in the early 1970s, one job was not enough, so B soon had a second job to support her brood of five growing children. She earned money for her family, and the older children, Curtis and Vera, learned how to step in and take over at home when B wasn't there. Vera gave up fighting for helping at home.

"I used to be a whiner, but when Mama had two jobs to make ends meet after Daddy died, I was cooking dinner when I was 14 for all the kids. Curtis and I babysat and had rules that homework was to be done. When the porch light went on, the children were to come home for dinner. I'd get school clothes out, everything, just like Mama. I felt proud by doing that. It was where I got my joy. I learned that from my mama." What a testimony to Beatrice and Vera. She was following in her mother's footsteps by doing what had to be done without complaining, and self-respect followed.

Falling in love with her first husband when she was in high school was another Vera memory. With education as the priority of Beatrice and N.D. for their children, there was certainly no room for marrying. "I was, absolutely, not allowed to get married in high school."

Vera did, however, get married when she graduated and gave Beatrice her first grandbaby, Patrice, who helped care for my mother, went to El Centro, and got a nursing degree. She was valedictorian of her nursing graduating class and now works in a radiologist's office.

Nine years later, Vera gave birth to Rashad, who now lives and works in New York City. Later, Darsha was born. Vera, like her mother, adores her three children and is very proud of them.

Patrice, Vera's oldest child, was close to Beatrice. She loved spending time with her grandmother over the years and learned to be responsible, smart, and motivated just like Grandmama. Patrice often stayed with Beatrice on weekends when she was in high school and would be there when Todd and Tyler, Marvella's little twins, came over. If her grandmama had to work, Patrice or her mother would babysit.

Beatrice's servant heart passed to her girls. Vera worked in caregiving just like her mother. Marvella worked in caregiving just like her mother. Patrice worked in caregiving just like her grandmother, mother, and aunt. Vera, Patrice, and Marvella were part of the Jones's team that took care of my mother for eight years—three generations showing care and compassion to others.

Vera laughed out loud when she remembered things her mother used to say. If any of the kids or cousins would gain weight, Beatrice would look at them and tell it like it was. "You're too fat and your butt's too big." Sometimes her mother would add, "Your titties are too big too." As if they could do anything about that! Would Beatrice's comments hurt their feelings? No. Vera said they would laugh. Somehow Beatrice could speak her mind and not offend whomever she spoke to. That's one of the enchanting mysteries of this unique woman.

Vera recalled two conversations which showed how her mama responded to life's problems:

"Keep living. The older you get, you'll understand. Keep living." Vera still hears these words from her mama. If ever anything was wrong, "I was to keep on living."

Once Beatrice's shoulder was bothering her when Vera was home. "Mama, what's wrong with your shoulder?"

"It's arthritis."

"Well, Mama, what can we do?"

"Keep on living"

End of conversation.

Beatrice always did "keep on living." One December day, B and Mom had come over for the three of us to decorate my Christmas tree. The feel and smells of Christmas were in the air, and the warmth of having B and Mom there made it perfect. The day was cold, and the aroma of hot spiced tea permeated through the kitchen to the rest of the house. Christmas carols were playing, and Nat King Cole began singing "I'm Dreaming of a White Christmas." I was talking to Mom and happened to look over at B.

There she was in her own world of Nat King Cole as he sang. B had begun swaying back and forth, humming softly. She felt the music, and her face was radiant as she looked far away. She was a vision to see, unaware of Mom and me for those few minutes. That was a special moment. I pictured Beatrice dancing years ago with N.D. to Nat King Cole.

Todd remembered his grandmama saying one time, "Oh, I love Nat King Cole—but I don't like his hair—the way he wears it all slicked back." B had her favorite celebrities, who also included Sidney Poitier and President Obama.

Aging is part of Beatrice's story. I'm pretty sure that if I told B I was sad she was getting older and not feeling well, she would have said something like, "That's silly. I'm old. I'm sick. Sick's sick. People get sick. Someday I'll die. We all will. So quit being sad about that."

Vera took care of her mother when she first needed help in her 80s. One of the great things about Vera is her strength. She could lift my mother out of bed or into a chair, and she did the exact same for her beloved mother.

Thinking about her mama, then 86 years old with diabetes,

high blood pressure, and dementia, Vera became somber. "Mama's a fighter right now. She always said, 'Get outta the bed and move around.' She knows to take her medicine. Yes, the dementia makes me sad, very sad. I can't ever think that she wouldn't know me."

21

"Just Walk on By"

Marvella Jones Atkins became the primary caregiver for her mother. Beatrice Jones spent almost 70 years raising and caring for children, grandchildren, and great-grandchildren, and great-great-grandchildren. She spent over 60 years caring for patients at Parkland and St. Paul's Hospital, patients in nursing homes, and home patients who could not care for themselves. That part of Beatrice's life ended when she was in her 80s. She became the one who needed care.

Vera cared for her mother with heart and soul until the house on Gillette sold, and the responsibility passed to B's younger daughter, Marvella. As stubbornly independent as Beatrice Jones always was, she accepted this transition in her life with dignity and grace.

Marvella is a lovely and compassionate woman. A physical therapist and nurses' aide were eventually needed to help care for Beatrice and give Marvella much needed relief. She'd begun working for my mother at night on the weekends, so I'd gotten to know her, but we became close friends through the years Beatrice lived in Marvella's home.

Marvella told the story of how she came to be called by two different names. "My birth certificate says I'm "Marshella," but my family and friends always called me Marvella. When I graduated from high school, they asked what name I wanted on my diploma. I wanted Marvella, but it would have cost more to have Marvella on the diploma since my birth certificate says Marshella. So my diploma says Marshella, but I'm called Marvella." She's both.

Marvella is married to Tennell Atkins. B had erratic hours of sleep and often enjoyed watching TV at 3:00 or 4:00 in the morning. She and Tennell would watch reruns together at these odd hours. They had a comfortable and trusting relationship. Tennell teased her about his taking over the famous blue chair that was the only place B wanted to sit. B would laugh and say, "Nope. This is my chair."

Marvella was handed the mantle of caregiving. I had asked B what she would do when her home sold. "I want to live with Marvella." She was comfortable and secure with Marvella and Tennell. Caring for a mother who cared for you is a privilege, but it is hard and exhausting work. Marvella did it day after day after day.

One day I'd mentioned to Todd that his mother sounded pretty exhausted with her caregiving duties the last time I'd spoken with Marvella. Todd laughed his warm laugh and knowingly responded, "And, Mary, she wouldn't have it any other way."

Marvella has shared stories of Beatrice's childhood, marriage, kids, years of loss, times of health challenges, years of impossible schedules, and insight into Beatrice's personality. Without her recall, so many stories of B would one day be lost. Marvella's first-hand memories added color, depth, and enrichment to learning more of Beatrice Jones's story.

Marvella has a lighter tone of black skin. When she was telling me about her mother's heritage in one conversation, she shared that her "great-great-grandfather had married an Oriental woman and, as far as I know, settled in Clarksville in Haywood, the black section of Clarksville." From this mixed marriage, a light-colored gene was passed down. Three of Beatrice's children, Curtis, Don, and Marvella, were born with this lighter tone of black skin.

The physical trait of lighter black skin was often hurtful to Marvella. She endured cruel teasing for years that was devastating for a young girl. She remembers her family being called the "village people" because of the variation of skin tone within her family. Marvella would cry, and Don would fight. Beatrice told them, "Just let it go."

It hurt Marvella deeply when she would hear comments like "did your mother jump the fence?" A sensitive child found out early how mean people can be, but she had just the mother to toughen her up.

"People might say to my mom because we had a different color of black skin, 'Are those your colored children?'"

My mother would look at them and say, "My children have a name." Beatrice had the zingers that could shut people up and knew when to use them. She knew when to assert herself and assert herself she would do when it involved her children.

"We were called 'nigger' all the time. Mama always said, 'Just hold your head up and be who you are. Keep walking.'" Marvella remembers these pieces of advice as if they had been spoken yesterday.

Beatrice worked at Parkland and got to know some of the doctors who became sources of good physicians for her children's medical care. Marvella remembers an instance when B had taken her children to see the dentist. Some in the waiting room began muttering to each other, "Who do those niggers think they are?" It would surprise no one to have heard Beatrice turn around and say to her children, "Just let it go. Ignorance has no place."

Beatrice's solutions to problems of racial mistreatment seemed to come naturally for her, but they imparted wisdom to others. Her children still echo Beatrice's simple, yet wise solution, all some version of "just let it go." These responses were repeated over and over, day after day, year after year; today they are ingrained in her children's hearts and minds. Beatrice Jones knew well what she could control and what she could not control. She could control her responses; she could not control the racism that surrounded her and her family. When she could not control, she "just let it go."

Although the years of segregation, racism, and blatant civil rights injustices continued into the 1950s, '60s, and '70s when B's children were growing up, they were able to get through these times without giving up because of their mother's strong support and simple wisdom. Beatrice took care of what was in front of her and expected her children to do the same, even when extremely difficult. She raised independent children with tools to use as adults dealing with the real world.

Some of Beatrice's solutions for her children when they were called "nigger" or heard mean or cruel comments may have seemed like short-term solutions then, but they were tools with which to approach adult life when things were beyond control.

"Just walk on by. Why pay attention to ignorant people?"

"Keep moving. Just keep moving."

"Just let it go."

"Just walk on by."

"Just hold your head high. You know who you are. Walk on by."

"Keep a-steppin'."

Beatrice Jones lived her life following her own advice.

In spite of often simple solutions, Marvella learned from her mother there are times to act. Beatrice's actions were never loud or raucous, but they were impactful. Her protests were quiet, dignified, and deliberate. Her protests involved few words but words that were remembered. Her protests were always about self-respect and dignity. Christianity was her bedrock and the example by which she strived to live. In turbulent years, Beatrice's Christianity was quiet strength and knowing who she was. Her parents and Jesus were her example.

B took two buses to work each day to Parkland. The first bus took her downtown; then she waited for another bus to get her to Parkland. She repeated this at the end of her work-day, sometimes returning home at night. Marvella fondly remembers walking down the street when she was young and hiding in the bushes to wait for her mother's bus if B were returning after dark.

If B wasn't working back to back jobs, occasionally Marvella would go downtown, meet her mother after work, and ride the bus home with her. She recalls a brave and memorable incident that occurred one afternoon.

"When I met Mama downtown, there were certain stores we could go in and some we couldn't because they didn't allow black people. We would sometimes go into Titche's for an ice cream cone and always go to the back of the counter so we could be served. For a while, we did this. One day Mama refused to go to the back of the counter."

When Beatrice would not budge, the server told her, "I can't serve you here. You need to go on to the back of the counter."

Beatrice responded, "My money's just as good as anybody else's right here, so I guess you can serve me right here."

"I can't serve you here."

"Well . . . then I'll just sit at a table," as B moved toward a table.

The server looked befuddled, probably because he hadn't had that happen to him before. He finally stuttered, "I didn't mean for you to go sit at a table."

"I'm too tired to move, and I'm stayin' here." Beatrice had drawn her line in the sand.

Marvella said, "I didn't know what would happen, but he brought us our ice cream cones. Mama thanked him. Later on after that, he would bring us burgers. Mama stood her ground when, one too many times, they tried to push her aside. This happened the same way it had at the barbecue shack in Clarksville."

The way in which Beatrice challenged wrong that day at Titche's earned respect from the server—and maybe a change in how he treated his black customers and black people in general. Beatrice was respectful to the server and thanked him when he brought Marvella and her their ice cream. B never had to say she believed in respect and manners. She lived that way.

These are courageous stories of Beatrice's quiet strength in the face of injustice. She did not have to prove her worth to anyone. She knew her worth as God's child. She and N.D. passed this attitude of pride tempered with humility, strength tempered with love, and actions tempered with wisdom and common sense to their children.

N.D.'s protests were more colorful than his wife's. He was

a valuable employee in the construction business. Marvella described her father as "a man of very few words and very stern. He worked with a lot of Anglos and could get angry. In certain situations, he would leave a job. He could do that because he was good at what he did and would get another job. Once his boss said something ugly to him, and my dad kicked him in the behind." Marvella was told the conversation between the two men went something like this:

"Nathan Jones, don't you come back!"

"I'll see you Monday morning, and I want my paycheck on time." Nathan went back on Monday, received his paycheck, and continued to work with the same boss.

Urbanization after the war brought blacks living together in close proximity. Injustices of racism that had been festering for years began boiling over. Whites in Dallas and the South resisted social change. The federal government stepped in and passed the Civil Rights Act that mandated change, but the majority of whites stuck in their white supremacy thinking made change difficult to implement. These were turbulent years in Dallas. Far-sighted leadership from Mayor Erik Jonsson and others plus a determined black population forged ahead to implement the law. City leaders worked to calm an angry city and improve morale.

Dallas struggled with the social changes occurring in the 1950s and 1960s. Integration of schools was made law in 1954, and the Civil Rights Act was passed in 1964. All five of Beatrice and Nathan Jones's children were born in the 1950s, which meant they were in school during these tumultuous times. Dallas had been a segregated city with designated colored and white schools, restrooms, residential areas, water fountains, restaurants, stores, barber shops, trains, and buses.

Integration of schools solved one problem and created

another. This change was hard on all students but hardest on black students entering a white world. Marvella explained, "Yes, it was extremely frightening. Mama walked me to school in first grade. Roger T. Mills Elementary had lots of whites and was one of the first to integrate. I looked sorta white, so I think that may have made it easier. By the end of my going there, the white school was almost all black because of white flight."

Curtis, Don, and Marvella were Beatrice's children with the lighter black skin. Marvella was young, and elementary school was not too difficult for her when schools integrated. Curtis, the oldest, was taunted and teased and would run home from school. Don would fight. Marvella would cry.

Marvella's favorite memory in elementary school occurred in first grade. "My first-grade class was putting on a play. I knew Mama couldn't come because she was working. But when I was up there as we started our play, I looked up, and there was Mama sitting in the back of the room. I thought she was the most beautiful person I'd ever seen. She'd gotten off work to come see me." Marvella's eyes glowed at this precious memory of her loving mother.

High school was harder for Marvella because of integration. She recalled, "Curtis drove us to school. My dad had died, and he'd had a Cadillac. Because of the car, black students acted to us like 'oh, you think you're too good for us,' and white kids gave us a bad time. We were caught in the middle a lot because of stuff like that and because we were so light skinned."

Marvella remembered an abusive incident that occurred in the school cafeteria: "In the cafeteria one day Rickey and I sat down for lunch. The football team came over and threw milk cartons at us and at me, twelve to fifteen of them saying, 'Nigger, go to your place.'"

The black principal came up to us and said, "Don't you

know where you're supposed to sit? You have to learn to stay in your place."

"We didn't know. I called my uncle from school. I didn't call my mom because I didn't want to upset her, and she was working. My uncle came up and talked to the black principal calling him an 'Uncle Tom' for not standing up for the black students."

"Then the white principal talked to the coaches of the athletes, and, you know, a lot of the basketball players were black. The coaches told 'em, 'you have to learn to get along.' One of the basketball players, Bill Walters, wanted me to be his girlfriend. He told the other players and coach he would quit if the team didn't treat me right. They didn't want him to quit. He was a high-scorer and key basketball player. I became his girlfriend and Rickey, my younger brother, his best friend. Then we all became friends. . . ."

Marvella's interesting footnote to that experience was, "Later I taught seventh- and eighth-grade honors classes at Walker. When the principal walked in, I recognized him—it was the same black principal who wouldn't stand up for us in high school."

22

"It's My Money!"

Todd Atkins is Beatrice's grandson and the son of Marvella and Tennell Atkins. He has a twin brother, Tyler. They are 36 years old. Todd is the pastor at Salem Baptist Church in Dallas. I got to know Todd when he would come by my mother's apartment on Friday afternoons. B called Friday her "happy day" because it was payday. Todd began keeping her books after Beatrice had begun working every week for Mom. Having her trusted grandson do this job was a great relief since she worked all week, fulfilled commitments at church, and was so involved with her family.

I came each Friday afternoon to write B's check. Often Todd was there when I came by. He is a handsome young man with a kindly demeanor. His face and voice exude warmth. B would simply hand him her check. No conversation. Todd would stay about thirty minutes, making sure her finances were in order. B was vigilant about insurance payments, bills, and saving for her future. The trust Beatrice had in Todd told me much about this young man. Todd was quiet as he worked but always happy. He always spoke to my mother.

B told me one day she had needed something for her house and asked Todd for the money. Todd told her she couldn't afford it.

"Oh, yes I can! It's my money, and I sure can. Give it to me." B got her money.

Todd had an even better version of the same story. He remembered somebody had come by the house selling alarm systems, and his grandmother wanted one. She told Todd she wanted money for the alarm system. Todd told her there wasn't enough money for her to do that. B let him have it. "It's only money. I ain't begged nobody for anything before, and I'm not gonna start now! Give me my money." B soon had her alarm system.

The way Beatrice spoke Todd's name came out as "Tard." So I called him "Tard." For three years, when I saw him, I would greet him, "Hi, Tard. How are you? Bye, Tard, have a nice week." At that time, Todd was chaplain at Methodist Hospital. One day, as he was leaving, I was standing in the kitchen and asked Tard for his card. Imagine my surprise when I looked at his business card and saw the name "Todd Atkins." Todd? I thought his name was Tard. I called Beatrice over and showed her his card.

"B, Tard's card says his name is Todd."

"That's right. His name is Tard. That's what it is."

"B, I'm confused. It's Todd. I've been calling him by the wrong name."

"Well, now you know." That was a typical B conversation. "Tard."

What an embarrassing mistake to mispronounce some-one's name every week for three years. If someone had called me by the wrong name week after week, I would have kindly explained the correct pronunciation of my name. It didn't bother Todd one bit. That is just like his grandmother. After three years, he became "Todd" to me—his real name!

When B cared for my mother, she often told stories of Reverend Campbell who was then pastor of Salem Baptist Church. He had been there for years, and B's relationship with Reverend and Mrs. Campbell was warm and familiar. Speaking of them reminded me of a story B once told me. I shared it with Todd.

One day, around 2006 or 2007, B seemed a little down. I asked her if she was okay. She told me Reverend Campbell had a stroke and was in the hospital. He never went back to the pulpit.

Interim pastors preached at Salem after Reverend Campbell. A year or so later, B told me, "The deacons have asked Todd to be the pastor at church." She had missed Reverend Campbell but now would be seeing her grandson in the pulpit. The church so close to B's heart had a new pastor, and it was her grandson. Beatrice beamed as much as Beatrice could beam.

"B, aren't you thrilled?"

"Yes, I am happy. I'm happy Salem has a pastor."

"Just happy? But B, it's Todd at Salem!"

"Yes, that's right. It's Tard." She smiled. She was proud. Very proud.

One Sunday morning in August, after the death of my mother, I picked B up at her house on Gillette. Since Todd was now the pastor of B's church that was so important to her, I asked if I might accompany her to church one Sunday. When I drove up, little Dymond, B's four-year-old great-great-grand-daughter was peeking through the front blinds. She ran in B's room exclaiming, "She's here. Mary Harris is here!" B always called me "Mary Harris" when she was talking to her family, and now little Dymond was doing the same thing.

Dymond would answer the phone, "Jones's residence," and I would ask if I could please speak with Beatrice. "Just a minute, please. I'll get her." I'd hear little footsteps and then, "Grandmama, telephone." Nothing like a four-year-old secretary to take your calls.

B just laughed as she told me about Dymond looking through the blinds. Then she said to me, "I wasn't sure if you'd come." I just rolled my eyes, and we headed to Salem Baptist. I couldn't wait.

Beatrice was all dressed up for church. She looked beautiful. I was proud to be her guest as we walked through the doors B had walked in so many times. We were seated on the fourth row, and I saw Todd sitting behind the pulpit. I felt proud of Todd too. Michelle, his wife, sat right behind us with adorable Baby Ella, then six months old. My friends would have oohed and gooed if their grandbaby was behind them, even in church. Not Beatrice. It might as well have been a stranger's baby. She was there to worship.

What a morning! I heard music from the choir different from the sedate white choirs in churches I'd attended. I heard drummers, guitarists, and gospel music. We sang hymns. The offering was passed, and I was proud as I put money in the basket for Salem. Later, Todd made an announcement for an offering that would help their college students who would soon leave for school and didn't have the money for books and supplies. The congregants were ushered row by row to a large basket at the front of the church to contribute to this cause. I whispered to B.

"B, there's another offering?"

"Yes, it's up there."

"But, B, I've already put money in the offering."

"It's time to put some more in."

"Well, B, you aren't going up there."

"I don't have any more money. But you do. I saw it in your purse. Now go on."

Same ole B. She was right. I did have more money in my purse. I walked forward and felt good, knowing I was helping a college student from Salem further his or her education. "B, will there be more offerings?"

"Maybe. Wait and see." She smiled at me.

B and I talked every couple of weeks after Mother died. She knew I missed my mom, and B missed her too. We both missed the afternoons of stories and visits with the three of us: Mom, B, and me. Whether the visits were funny, serious, or quiet, some wonderful history was made in those nine years.

B went to work pretty soon after Mother's death, thankfully. She'd been after me to find her a job, and a friend called needing help for her elderly father-in-law. B was almost 80 when she went back to work. Her new job was the last she'd have after nursing and caring for the ill and elderly for over 60 years.

Retiring in one's 80s? Not a surprise if you know Beatrice Jones. However, in a few months, B, herself, began not feeling well. One afternoon, I drove to her home on Gillette to see her. We visited in her home as she sat in Mom's blue chair. B's age was showing. Her body was tired.

I began to think about Beatrice a lot—the person, Beatrice. Not the friend, not the caregiver. Just Beatrice. I thought about the clarity with which she lived her life: a Christian faith she relied on daily and that had gotten her through much heartache, the love and devotion for her children and family, her friends and neighbors, giving her time and money to Salem

Baptist, generosity toward anyone in need, and always having a job and earning her own way. Those were B's priorities. She hadn't ever had the money or the desire to be taken in by things of the world.

B stayed on my mind. In a way, I was envious of the certainty and simplicity with which she lived her life. I wanted to know more about Beatrice Jones, a black woman for whom life had been hard but who lived most days with gratitude and joy. I knew whom to call.

The warmest message greeted me when I called Todd to ask him about his grandmother, Beatrice Dilworth Jones. "This is Reverend Todd Atkins of Salem Baptist Church. If you could, please leave your name, number, and a message, and I will be glad to call you back at my earliest convenience. May God bless you and keep you is my prayer. Thank you, and have a great day." Todd's sincerity and genuine caring come through in his resonant voice.

Todd Atkins is the pastor of Salem Baptist Church, in Pleasant Grove, where Beatrice has given almost half a century of her life worshipping on Sunday mornings, teaching and attending Sunday School, singing in the choir, participating in Daughters of Naomi on Wednesday nights, and cooking and serving meals. Salem has truly been Beatrice's second home.

Todd and I coordinated a time to visit so I could learn more about his grandmother. I read Todd's bio on the Salem Baptist website. He not only serves as Pastor Todd Atkins of Salem Baptist Church but also is employed by hospice to minister to the dying. He is active in the South Dallas community, serving in multiple organizations to improve black lives. He speaks to the Dallas City Council about needs in his community. Todd is working at his church to set up a nursery for children with working parents. Multiple jobs. Who does this sound like?

I asked Todd about his jobs and other ministries, his wife, Michelle, and their two children, Ella and Miles. Ella was four and Miles 18 months when we visited. Again, just like Beatrice, Todd's heart is given to God, his family, his church, and those who are hurting.

What respect I have for this young family. Todd is using his gifts to minister to church members and his community. Much of what he does is "behind the scenes," and he may not see the fruits of his efforts in his lifetime. That doesn't matter to him. Todd knows he is led by the Holy Spirit to do all he can to love and help God's children. Michelle is lovely and soft-spoken. She teaches music in an elementary school near Lemmon and plays the violin at church. Still with all they have on their plate, their priority is family. Every day of Beatrice's work was behind the scenes, never trying to impress. Just doing what needed to be done—exactly what Todd is doing now.

"Todd, how do you do all of this? Are you really doing all of these jobs?"

"Yes, I am."

"How? Day after day."

"Well, Mary, sometimes I lean against a real sturdy wall." Todd said that while laughing his warm, wonderful laugh.

Beatrice Jones would be proud of what her grandson is doing but not surprised. All is fine if someone "has a job," yet this job as well as extra efforts to help the dying and a community in need reflect the core values Beatrice held closest—her faith and desire to help others.

When Todd had come to my mother's apartment every week to get B's paycheck and work on her finances, he saw Mom's piano and knew how much she loved to play. I asked him what had happened to my mother's piano when Beatrice's house on Gillette sold. My brother and I had given the piano to B when our mother died. Mother had been a gifted pianist and music filled our home when we were young—everything from hymns, children's songs, every patriotic song ever written to "Twelfth Street Rag." Music was her gift, her love, her comfort. The piano had sat proudly in B's home with family pictures on the top. Todd knew that piano was a way for me to hold onto a wonderful part of my mother, and I hoped it wasn't gone.

Todd told me when the house sold, and everyone was taking all the furniture that he rescued Mother's piano, and now Marvella, his mother, has it. That pleased me because that meant the piano had stayed with Beatrice. That piano was an emotional bond between my mother and me, Beatrice and my mother, and Beatrice and me. The piano along with the well-known blue chair were the two pieces of furniture that were the most important to Mom at the end of her life.

Being a fairly new member of a large congregation and not knowing the pastors personally, I mentioned something to Todd I had given thought to for a while. I came right out and asked him my question. "Todd, I think I would like for you to do my funeral."

"Okay. Mary, that's the nicest compliment I could ever get. Just don't do it tomorrow."

Right there was B's quick wit and sense of humor. We laughed, and I told him I wouldn't, and I'd see him in a couple of days at Salem.

23

"Pay Your Bills and Get Saved"

On a pleasant summer morning, I arrived at Salem to meet with Todd. By this time, I wanted to know more than just how B was feeling. I wanted to find out more about the unique Beatrice Jones. Todd was gracious to give his time for me to learn more about his grandmother and met me with a smile and big ole bear hug. He ushered me into the sanctuary where he showed me the renovation that had been completed. He is proud of his church. He is proud of his grandmother's church where he grew up.

The old carpet in the chancel area had been ripped up. Hardwood floors underneath had been the exciting discovery. They were refinished and now are shiny and beautiful. The choir and music area were larger. The entire area could now accommodate a screen or a student performance. Church membership was growing, and these were years when church membership across the country was declining.

I was happy because Salem is home to Beatrice, and the church is alive and well. It still remains the close and involved church family B experienced, but today Salem has an energy that is responding to the 21st century.

The sanctuary is lovely, exuding a peace that made me want to sit here alone. I may come back and do that. The sanctuary is medium sized yet intimate. There are beautiful, square stained-glass windows that look like crowns atop wood plank walls.

What touched me most was when Todd showed me one of the stained-glass windows. By the side of it was a plaque that read, " In Memory of S. DILWORTH by B. JONES FAMILY." S. Dilworth is Searcey, Beatrice's father.

I was humbled. Beatrice has always been frugal but generous. I never knew her to have extra money. A stained-glass window would have been a big expense, but to her, it was a gift to the church she loved and a way to honor the memory of a father she loved, respected, and cared for in his last years. She made it a gift not just from herself but from the family. That's Beatrice.

The sanctuary was quiet and peaceful, and Todd ushered me to the front pew on the right side. I was quieted by sitting in Beatrice's church. "Mary, this is where Grandmama sat every Sunday after she moved in with Marvella." The right front pew could accommodate a wheelchair on the inside aisle, and Marvella would sit next to her. They would come for the last half of the service to hear the message and sing.

The entire service became too much for Beatrice. Proof of this was the comment she made one Sunday in the middle the church service to Marvella in a nonwhispered voice. What embarrassed Marvella that she heard from her mother was, "Time to get our asses outta here." Marvella quickly wheeled

B out before she could repeat her exit line. Half a service was obviously quite sufficient!

Todd acted as if he had all the time in the world to visit with me. He gave no indication of a busy day ahead. His demeanor was calm, a reflection of the calmness of the sanctuary where we sat. We chatted a minute, and then we began talking about B. I asked Todd how he would describe his grandmother.

"Witty. Blunt. Pillar of strength. Faith is her strongest thing. I've only seen her cry one time. That was when her brother, Sonny, died. Oh, she worried about him. He didn't give the Lord time. She wanted him to stop drinkin'. She and I would take turns going over cleanin' him up and takin' care of him."

I, too, remembered when Sonny died. B would talk about her brother and going to see about him. She would laugh about what a mess he was. No judgment, no complaining, only love and acceptance. Although Sonny drank, he was sick, and he was B's big brother. As a little girl, she could not say "Sonny," so he was always "Big Bud," and Beatrice was always "Lil' Sister." They kept these names till Sonny died—over 70 years. I did not know the impact Sonny's death had on B. I am sorry I didn't because I would have taken more time to show I cared for her loss and her pain.

I was quiet a minute, absorbing what I just learned from Todd. I wondered aloud what had impacted him most from his grandmother. He laughed such a knowing laugh. "Two things. Pay your bills and get saved."

B's greatest pain in life had to be burying two young sons. I knew Curtis had died of a brain tumor. Nothing specific had ever been said about Don's death. B never said anything that would cast a negative light on one of her children. I thought Don had been killed in a shooting at a gas station. According to Todd, I was incorrect.

Todd loved his uncle but told me Don had lived a rough life. There was no judgment in his voice either. In Todd's matter-of-fact and kind voice, I learned a different story and the heartache B had endured. Todd said in his matter-of-fact, kind voice, "Don was involved with drugs, alcohol, gambling . . . and Mary, he was a pimp." My eyes widened.

Todd smiled as he remembered an incident where Beatrice had enough with Don's shenanigans. "Don's at the house fighting with one of his girls in the driveway. Grandmama told me she was gonna run him down. She got in the car and drove up the driveway. Don jumped. Then she turned the water hose on him." Beatrice finally told Don, "I just have to put you in the hands of the Lord." She did. Don was found dead in a car one night.

"Grandmama was shocked and not shocked. The life he lived . . . . Police came to her house and told her. She couldn't go down there, to the morgue. Mr. Franklin, a neighbor, said, 'I'll take care of it.' He did what needed to be done." Todd paused as he remembered.

"Don had light skin, well, and a sandy afro." Caught off guard by the sandy afro, I smiled and tried to picture Don. Todd continued, "He got teased so much, and he fought. That's how he got to be such a good fighter." Todd smiled, too, as he remembered his uncle's sandy afro.

Todd shifted to talking about Curtis. "Curtis had been a substitute teacher in DISD and was so good, he was hired permanently. He and Vera had been their mother's right arm when she was working two jobs and still had young children at home. Curtis drove the children to school and wherever else they needed to be. Vera cooked dinner."

Todd explained how Curtis, his uncle, taught him, his brother, and other kids to read while sitting in his grandmama's living room. He smiled fondly as he remembered the book that had a parrot on the front.

At age 29, Curtis began not feeling well and was diagnosed with a brain tumor. Beatrice nursed him at home until his death. As Todd and I sat on that front pew of Salem Baptist in the quiet, he pointed out, ten feet away, where the caskets had been at different times holding the bodies of a husband and two sons. I just stared where those caskets had been placed years before. In less than a decade, B had buried her husband, two sons, and her parents. Beatrice, a wife and mother, had sat just a few feet away saying goodbye to those she loved, N.D., Curtis, and Don, much too early.

Beatrice Jones grieved deeply over these losses but refused to wallow in her grief. Her mother's heart was heavy, but grief would not beat Beatrice. Her faith was stronger than death. Beatrice trusted the Lord to know the best for His children's lives no matter what that held. Her faith was like a rock that never moved. She always said her job was to "keep moving" and keep moving she did, even when the blows kept coming. Beatrice Jones never quit.

Todd looked back on 34 years of knowing his grandmother. "Grandmama was a pillar of strength." He thought back to when his grandmother had an aneurysm, and the doctors told her "she'd never walk again, never take care of herself again."

B, supposedly, had said right back to the doctors, "Shoot, as long as I'm here, I'll be working. Then I'll die."

"Never tell Grandmama she couldn't do something. She was unbreakable."

Growing up during the Depression and racist years of the 1930s and 1940s and seeing how her parents dealt with poverty, uncertainty, and feeding and caring for eight children gave Beatrice a model. Much was required of the children on the farm, and this developed a work ethic and strength that only toughened Beatrice, not only in her childhood but also all through her life.

A warm smile crossed Todd's face at the memory of his great-grandparents. "My grandmother was like her father. Searcey would work from sunup to sundown. He was playful and stern. Searcey could put a square peg in a round hole all day long. Grandmama took after him."

Then Todd chuckled. "My grandmother, Ophelia, was a neat freak, wearing white gloves when she went out and washing her greens with soap. She wouldn't eat no one's cooking but her own. That's probably why Grandmama is such a good cook."

24

Fryin' Chicken

Sunday was always church day at Grandmama's when Todd was growing up and staying there on weekends. "Grandmama would go to church, sing in the choir, either teach or go to Sunday School, then have the family over for Sunday dinner about 3:00 in the afternoon."

"They all come," Beatrice told me once, and Todd confirmed. "There would be about 30 of us." B cooked it all. Todd smiled big as he remembered, "Apple cake and carrot cake were her specialties. I still remember the brown paper she'd lay out to make the cake on. Same ole brown paper."

I asked Todd how she had the energy to do all that on Sundays after working all week. At one point, she didn't. It had become too much. Todd smiled at this memory. Beatrice called him one day proclaiming, "I am cuttin' this shit out!" And she did. No more Sunday afternoon dinners.

Once Beatrice made me an apple cake simply because I asked. I knew about the apple cakes her family loved. I hadn't really expected B to do this, but she did. I now know she spread it out on the famous brown paper she'd used for her family over and over when baking for them. My apple cake was delicious, every bite tasting of B's home cooking. I pictured her in her kitchen baking just for me, and I am touched by her loving gift.

Todd and Tyler spent every weekend with Beatrice when they were boys. "We always wanted to go and play with Patrice and Rashad, Vera's children. My parents would drop us off Friday afternoon. We'd stay all day Saturday and Sunday. . . . My grandmother ran a tight ship.

When Grandmama worked, Vera or Patrice would be in charge. We'd do everything—climb on the roof, jump from the garage roof to the house roof. Once we wanted to earn some money and went door to door asking people if we could mow their yards, but you know, you have to have a lawn mower to do that. We were not supposed to leave the house, and Vera whipped us."

One of Todd's favorite stories was when he and Tyler were at B's on another weekend. Beatrice's father, Searcey, was also there since she continued to care for him after her mother died.

"Grandmama didn't drive, and one Saturday she walked to the drugstore to get some things for her dad. Tyler and I thought she was gone too long. We were about five. We took off in our pajamas to find her. We made it to the 7-11, and the lady recognized us and called the police to take us home. When we drove up in the police car, Tyler was so excited, he pointed and said, 'Look, there's Grandmama!' She was frantic, thought somebody 'had stole us.' Then she was mad. My daddy came and got us, picked one up in one hand, one in the other. Worse beatin' I ever got." Todd was laughing the entire time he told this story. He has wonderful, warm, and vivid memories of times spent with his grandmama at church and at her house.

As young children, Todd and Tyler spent all day Saturday at church when Beatrice was helping prepare food to serve on the Sundays church members gathered for a meal. "Grandmama and another lady would drive down to Pilgrim's Pride, buy crates of chickens, come back, clean and cut them, then fry every one of those chickens. This took most of the day.

"We'd all play here at church and have choir practice too. It was fun. Then on Sunday, we'd go to church. Grandmama would always give us a quarter for a donut. We had our offering envelopes too. There would be church, Sunday School, lunch, and an afternoon service or night service." Church was an all-day affair at Salem Baptist. Todd continually smiled as he remembered those wonderful days with his grandmother and cousins.

Since children, grandchildren, great-grandchildren, and great-great-grandchildren spent a lot of time with their grandmama, they had a chance to absorb character traits of Beatrice and later, as adults, to emulate qualities they'd observed in her. Generosity is universally mentioned throughout Beatrice's family. Her generosity wasn't showy, nor did she speak of it. But her family knows it. I know it. So many were all recipients of her generosity one way or another.

"Grandmama's house was never empty. Someone was always staying with her between jobs or needed a place to stay." Todd remembers his grandmother telling people, "I've got wall-to-wall carpet so there's always room to sleep on the floor." That sounds just like Beatrice. Even in her 70s, B let people stay with her.

Everyone knew B had her limits. One day Beatrice called

Todd when she "had it" with people taking advantage of her generosity. She was fed up and told him, "They've used up all my toilet tissue! Let 'em just wipe their ass with Kleenex!"

B told me a story about another time she'd "had it" with someone staying in her house taking advantage. This time, her solution was a bit more extreme than Kleenex. She called in a carpenter and had the wall between her bedroom and the occupied bedroom behind her knocked out. "That person is now gone, and I have a nice, big new bedroom. I can stand in my house and say, 'Peace in the Valley.'"

B's lack of fear to take action or speak up when the time was right reminded Todd of B's favorite cuss word. "Mary, you need to know Grandmama's favorite cuss word. It's 'shit.'" I laughed because I knew that. I'd heard her say "shit" if she dropped something, burned something, or spilled in the kitchen. B spoke her word so naturally, and not often, and I never heard her apologize. She didn't need to. "Shit" seemed appropriate speech the way B said it. But she would never say it in front of my mother. Or maybe she did since my mother couldn't hear.

Thinking about Beatrice's generosity of letting people stay or live in her house reminded me of a time when I'd talked about feeling lonely to B. "Mary, I just close my door when people leave, and I say, 'Peace in the Valley.' I lean against that front door and just breathe and say it again, 'Peace in the Valley.'" Being by herself, after all her hospitality to others, was a relief. Or if company hadn't even been around, she'd sometimes say, "Peace in the Valley." The walls in my home began hearing, "Peace in the Valley."

I pictured B's home full of noisy family all together with her either cooking in her kitchen, issuing orders, or laughing with them. Then I pictured earlier days with all the grandchildren spending afternoons, weekends, or several weeks with their grandmother. She loved having the "babies" over, and they loved being at her house. There are many memories from those days spent with Grandmama. Even in her late 70s and early 80s, B kept great-grandchildren and great-great-grandchildren at her house and ran as tight a ship as ever.

I looked at this man, once a boy, who spent every weekend with his grandmother and who sat in her church that he now pastors. I began to wonder how Todd chose the ministry as his profession. I knew he had graduated with a master's degree from Perkins School of Theology and that when I'd first met him, he was chaplain at Methodist Hospital. His answer to my question was immediate but not surprising. He gave all the credit to Beatrice, his grandmama.

"I wouldn't be a pastor without Grandmama. She had us in church every Sunday. I wanted to go into ministry in high school. My first year in college, I knew. . . . Then one day, after Reverend Campbell had his stroke, I was at church vacuuming up in front. The head of the deacons came up and asked me to ride with him. We got in his car, drove, and he stopped in the parking lot of a grocery store. He turned and asked me if I'd like to pastor the church—did I think I could do it. I told him I thought I could. That's how it happened." Todd was about 30 years old. B was working for my mother and about 76 years old. Her grandson had just become pastor of the church she loved and the church where she had taken her grandson and his twin brother every weekend as little boys.

Today Todd preaches from the pulpit of the church that was once his playground and a place to get a donut.

25

"Shut Up, Baby"

Patrice, Vera's daughter and Beatrice's first grandchild, has the work ethic and judgment of her grandmother. She is delightful to visit with and has a wonderful sense of humor, yet she is not as outwardly assertive as her grandmother. Not many are. Patrice, Vera, and Marvella were the backup shifts for my mother when Beatrice went home. Patrice was as dependable as the sun coming up. She has three children, went back to school for a nursing degree, and is now working in a doctor's office.

Patrice had a full-time life as a wife and mother of three children when employed to help my mother. With all of that, she made a decision to further her education, enrolling at El Centro in nursing. She managed all of this and still was never late or canceled when she worked for my mother.

Patrice graduated valedictorian of her El Centro class. I saw the pride on her mother's and grandmother's faces as they watched Patrice walk in with her fellow graduates to the stately music of "Pomp and Circumstance." She sat at the center of the stage looking beautiful in her cap and gown.

Since Patrice is quiet and soft-spoken, it might seem she would have been nervous giving a speech. Not so. Patrice was always calm about what was in front of her, just like her grandmother. Her speech to her class was confident and encouraging. Graduation Day was a wonderful day for the family honoring Patrice after years of study and hard work. Multiple family members were there to honor her. I was too.

Each family member was dressed in his or her Sunday finest. As we seated ourselves and the ceremony would soon begin, a typical interaction involving Beatrice went unnoticed, except by me. B and I were sitting together, and one of the family members sitting behind us was holding a baby. The baby began making noise—unacceptable on this special occasion. Beatrice took care of the situation easily with only three words. She turned, looked right at the wiggly baby and instructed, "Shut up, Baby." The baby looked at her and got quiet. B turned back around, and her attention was once more on the stage. Beatrice would not be disturbed from her granddaughter's graduation ceremony by anyone, adult or baby.

Patrice and Beatrice were close. Patrice respected her grandmother's deep wisdom and was saddened at seeing her grandmother lose her independence. Patrice will always have wonderful memories of their times together.

Another devoted grandchild is Rashad, Vera's second child and Patrice's younger brother. Rashad sings. He always sang. Patrice remembered that he would sing at an early age all the time. She chuckled, "We fibbed that he was good at first. Then he was good. He went to Booker T. Washington for the Talented and Gifted and now lives in New York singing."

He's also been a wedding planner and a wardrobe consultant for TV. With high profile jobs, Rashad still came home twice a year, and once was always on Beatrice's birthday, April 9. Beatrice's family was devoted to her wherever they were.

Beatrice loved each and every one of her grandchildren, no matter who or what generation. All have spent time with her in her home. B's home seemed to be the drop-off place for a needed babysitter. No matter the number, all were welcome. Some, including Patrice and Marvella's twins, Todd and Tyler, have almost grown up at their grandmama's house because of Sunday family dinners and spending days and nights with Beatrice. No matter how much time, all have heard Grandmama's wisdom, admonishments, and laughter.

As Patrice was close to her grandmother, it is no surprise Patrice's daughter, Kyisha, was too. She could be Beatrice's clone even though she's a great-granddaughter. Kyisha proudly said, "I'm my grandmama's mini-me." Those two did have a special bond. B would chuckle even when Kyisha's name came up with no story at all. She called her "Isha."

I don't know how to say it diplomatically, so I will speak as B would; Kyisha is a pistol. Kyisha is bossy. Kyisha takes charge. She was an 11-year-old adult, and especially so with her grandmother, as I realized when I'd hear stories about their time together. 'Isha always wanted to take care of Beatrice, her grandmama.

B got so tickled as she told this story. Kyisha had been at her grandmother's house and was getting ready to go home. She began tightly closing all the blinds at B's house. It was about 5:00 in the afternoon, and the sun was still out. "'Isha, what are you doing?"

"Grandmama, I'm getting ready to go, and you have to be safe. I'll take care of things." B left it alone and delighted in her take-charge 11-year-old great-granddaughter.

One day, Beatrice and Kyisha had taken B's car to get an estimate for bodywork. The man came out, studied the problem while rubbing his chin, did his calculating on a pad of paper, and gave Beatrice the estimate. B was thinking about the cost when 'Isha stepped in. Kyisha looked at the man and said, "That price seems a little high for my grandmother. She doesn't have a lot of money. We need you to come down on the price." Beatrice, for once, was caught off-guard. She laughed and laughed, as I did, at this funny little girl who spoke as an adult negotiating a business deal. No matter the age, Beatrice's family took care of their matriarch.

I felt I knew Kyisha by now from B's stories. I came by Mom's one afternoon and greeted B and Mom. We were all visiting, and B began to grin. Kyisha was about 14. B began, "I went to 'Isha's basketball game Saturday." For a minute, she couldn't continue because she got so tickled. "'Isha is now playing basketball, and I'd gone to watch her. That girl took the ball away from everybody, even her own teammates. She thought she was running the show, playing and coaching." B just shook her head and kept chuckling. From what B told me, my guess would be Kyisha could run the show or, at the very least, think she could.

Two other instances of Kyisha's engaging personality entertained Beatrice. 'Isha often spent the weekend with her grandmother, and of course, Sunday morning was for church. Paper and pencil in hand, this young girl was prepared and took notes during the sermon, just as if she were in school. B had never seen this. As she got older, Kyisha was in the choir. With the heart and soul with which members of Salem Baptist sang, the youth choir upped that even more. And 'Isha? B said her choir all danced when they sang, but "no one danced like

'Isha!" B cracked up each time she thought of times at church with her granddaughter.

Kyisha is now out of college and substituting in Plano schools. Whatever grade she is teaching, I guarantee they love her, and she is in charge. I was thrilled when Kyisha and I got in touch with each other. I told her that I was writing a book about her great-grandmother because I admired her so much. I knew this little girl, now a young woman, would have a story.

"I'm actually writing a book also. I'm in the brainstorming process so good timing. I will get back to you. I have to think back on a story." Two people wanting to write a book on Beatrice aka Grandmama. What interesting and different perspectives from which we would each write. 'Isha had an extraordinarily close relationship with her grandmother, and every time B talked about her, the love and pride in her eyes showed as she'd smile or die laughing. She loved this little girl, and Kyisha loved her. They were quite a pair together. Now a young woman, Kyisha settled back into remembering earlier years with her grandmother, thinking about the impact Beatrice had on her life.

"My grandmother has always been an inspiration plus motivation to me. She raised me basically. She's the reason I'm so amazing. A few things that stuck with me were her hard work and strength. I know she was always dedicated to working two jobs, if not more, to provide for her family, even before I was born. She often told me stories of how she would have to walk from one job to the next sometimes and catch the bus a lot because she had no transportation."

"She was advising me at all times to be grateful for the small things I have. She pushed herself no matter what, and that is something that resides within me. I get my drive from her. She was so funny; there was never a dull moment with her. She could make me 'cry-laugh' from the smallest jokes. I can also remember she would always teach me things such as crafting, sewing, baking, and cooking when I would spend the weekends with her. It was always constant learning of how to create things naturally."

Kyisha told about the difficulty of adjusting to college and calling her grandmother almost every day. "Grandmama would tell me, 'Keep a-steppin.'" Beatrice's philosophy in dealing with hard times has been repeated from every family member with whom I've spoken, just different phrasing this time.

Beatrice had lots of 'Isha stories but told stories about her other grandchildren too. One Monday, she began chuckling as she thought about the previous weekend. B and her family were going to a wedding that Saturday. She was dressed and ready to leave for the wedding. I'd seen B dress up for special occasions, and she always looked beautiful—so put together and different from her nurse uniforms and Christmas sweatshirt that I frequently saw. This particular Saturday, she had on a dress that had a V-neck.

Her little grandson was standing by her as everyone readied themselves before leaving. This little boy frowned as he studied his grandmama. He was concerned. Beatrice's beautiful dress exposed more of his grandmother than he was used to seeing. He wanted to help her cover up so much décolletage. It was only a minute before he had the answer. This little boy looked up, optimistically, at Beatrice with his big brown eyes and offered his solution. "Grandmama, I'm going get a piece of paper, and you can put it right up there in your dress," as he pointed to her exposure of skin. He ran off to save the day for Grandmama. B was greatly amused, thanked him, and didn't wear her paper accessory, but she loved this story. What I saw was the love and desire to protect his grandmother, no matter the problem.

All the children, grandchildren, great- and great-great-grandchildren have memories of Grandmama. My four children do too. They got to know Beatrice well during the years she spent with their grandmother. They would visit with Mama T and B when they could. The situations in which my children knew Beatrice were different from Kyisha's and B's other family members, but all saw a version of the same Beatrice—just different stories.

Jenny is my younger daughter and Mama T's most frequent visitor since she was in Dallas. Jenny shares a trait of Beatrice's that has endeared Beatrice to every person for whom she has cared. This unique gift is being able to relate to a sick or elderly patient or someone with a disability with not only kindness but also a camaraderie of respect, caring, and reassurance. Confidence and peace for the aging and sick are not patented medications.

I watched my mother, even as the clouds of dementia and depression began to enfold her, respond with conversation and laughter when talking with Jenny. Beatrice responded the same with Jenny. However, because B was there all day, she knew much of the time that my mother desired quiet, and she respected that. Mom was comfortable with both of these women. She loved Jenny, and she loved Beatrice.

The politically correct gene bypassed my daughter. Jenny and her politically incorrect personality coupled with Mother and her proper code of conduct were a delightful duo to observe when they were together. My mother delighted in Jenny's visits. Jenny could tease her grandmother with just the right degree of respect and sensitivity, causing my mother to get so tickled at Jenny, at me, or at herself.

If Mother asked Jenny her plans for Saturday, Jenny might respond she was planning to stay out all night. My mother would get so tickled, knowing that wasn't true, when in reality . . . . Jenny spoke to her grandmother not as an infirm elderly person but as adult to adult, peer to peer.

At one point in her young life, Jenny was discouraged about not finding work and talked to Mama T about her situation. One morning, after B had retrieved the newspaper for Mom, she quietly watched as my mother combed the employment section of *The Dallas Morning News* searching job opportunities for Jenny. This was a time when young people were using only the internet for job opportunities and applications. A newspaper with ads for employment was passé.

Jenny walked in and saw her grandmother marking ads with the newspaper. This effort from her grandmother to help her tickled Jenny but also touched her deeply. She called me, and we shared a laugh at this dear and loving effort of a grandmother to help her granddaughter.

My mother cared about her grandchildren having a job, B cared about her children and grandchildren having jobs, and now Jenny cared about having a job. Jenny has never forgotten that loving gesture of her 92-year-old grandmother, even recalling it at Mama T's funeral. Both Beatrice and Jenny never saw a need to show an elderly person the new ways. That is respect.

Jenny spoke comfortably and honestly to her grandmother just as Beatrice did. Jenny gave the gift of making her elderly grandmother feel important and needed. Beatrice gave that gift daily. Beatrice and Jenny had that special repartée that never imparted a "poor you" to an elderly or sick person. B enjoyed listening to the interactions between my mother and Jenny.

One day as Jenny was thinking about Beatrice, she said, "Mom, B was loving, even though she was sort of a 'take no prisoners' no-nonsense personality." My daughter began talking, and I was touched listening to her insight. Jenny continued, "You know, underneath, like her whole 'that doesn't bother me,' B is very kind taking care of people. I think that's not a front, but don't be fooled by her toughness . . . . You know, no senior citizen wants to be cared for or be dependent, yet what kind of caregiver is it that the one being cared for calls the caregiver her best friend?" Jenny nailed it.

Jenny's irreverent sense of humor coupled with her sensitive nature can be a confusing mix. Beatrice delighted in Jenny just as she did Kyisha. Jenny had come by one day to visit and later said, "I'd gotten my hair cut and dyed. B looked at it and didn't say, 'Oh, it's cute,' but said something that I, as sensitive as I am, would have reacted to. But with B, it didn't bother me." Beatrice Jones never would have said "it's cute" if she didn't think so. At least, with Jenny, that day B reined in any comments.

I, Mary Harris, wish I had B's secret. Never did she walk on eggshells, nor was she unkind. She spoke factually or what was factual to her. As Todd said, "She is blunt." Her "victims" seemed never to be offended, maybe because what she said was true or contained a grain of truth. Beatrice spoke with no judgment. She just spoke. I still cannot figure it out.

Sally is my mother's other granddaughter and my older daughter. Sally lived out of town but when in town made time to see her grandmother. One of the most thoughtful things she did was give Mama T a manicure if "the sisters," B and Mom, hadn't made it to the Vietnamese nail salon. Even if they had, Mama T preferred Sally's manicure any day. She'd ask Sally to take off her fresh polish, that she hadn't really liked the color anyway. Giving an elderly mother or grandmother a manicure was a gift of time and love from Sally.

The summer before her senior year, Sally dove into a swimming pool and had a serious neck injury that put her in the hospital. This was a very scary time. I'd had a major back surgery four months prior and was still in a back brace with strict warnings to take it easy. My husband was working, and I was at the hospital with Sally during the day. After a few days, the back pain began, and I knew I had to have some relief.

I called B. "Hi, Beatrice. This is Mary." That's what I always said.

"I know who it is," she would say with a chuckle. That was what B always said. Beatrice got serious when I told her the situation. "Yes, tell me the room number, and I'll be there tomorrow at 3:00 or 4:00, as soon as I get off my other job." Once more, B took two jobs, and it didn't faze her one bit.

Beatrice was a huge comfort to Sally and the only person with whom I would have left my daughter. To Sally and me, the memories of those days are clear. Way too clear. I remember Beatrice, once again, being my right arm. B hurt for Sally, and she hurt for me, as she would notice the pain and worry on my face.

Sally healed. She remembered Beatrice being right there for her. "Beatrice was a critical part of a recovery process for me. Before my senior year in high school, I had surgery after a scary diving accident. As I adjusted to limitations healing required, Beatrice's care and attention were part of my building the strength of heart I needed to not lose determination and take recovery one step at a time. Her presence was healing in and of itself. She was responsive, encouraging, and tender."

26

"Mr. Brown! You Can't Do That!"

Beatrice had a special relationship with two elderly men she cared for toward the end of her career—Mr. Brown and Dr. Jackson. She was with Mr. Brown for five years and Dr. Jackson for less than two years. Their families shared some wonderful stories of B during her years with these two fine men.

Mr. Brown was a sweet, kind man with two sons, Jack and Gilbert. B alternated weeks working for Mr. Brown and my mother. B would occasionally talk about Mr. Brown and funny things he'd said or that had happened when she was there.

Diamond, Mr. Brown's dastardly cat, was often the focus of Beatrice's anger. She talked a lot about that cat. Diamond got into B's way constantly. "Get outta here, Diamond!" was the most civilized command B could muster within hearing of Mr. Brown.

"Now B, don't be so hard on Diamond," kind Mr. Brown would say before he lost his ability to speak. His suggestion fell on deaf ears. B hated that cat and would even spray it with Lysol when Mr. Brown wasn't looking.

Jack has told one story about B and Mr. Brown, repeatedly, over the years. He calls the story "a classic" and still gets so tickled telling it, he can hardly talk. Finally in his slow Texas drawl, he began, once again, to tell his favorite story about B and his dad.

"B was in the kitchen cooking dinner one night. She went in to check on my dad and couldn't believe it. His lift chair was halfway up, and Dad was hangin' on for dear life and shakin' all over. B was obviously upset." Jack pictures his frail father, unable to walk or talk at that point, trying to stay in a chair that was rising off the floor. Jack can't help it—he starts laughing all over again at the bizarre picture of his helpless dad all but levitating.

"Oh, Mr. Brown! Mr. Brown! You can't do that!" Beatrice was really upset with him, thinking he'd tried to stand up on his own without her help and knowing he could have fallen out of the chair face forward, resulting in a serious injury or worse. B took the remote control for the chair and put it behind Mr. Brown where he couldn't reach it. She went back into the kitchen to finish preparing dinner.

"The same thing happened again. B's in there cookin', and my dad's back in the chair like he's supposed to be. B went in to check on him. Again, Dad's halfway up in the chair holding on for dear life and just shakin' and shakin'. B really scolded my dad."

"Mr. Brown! Stop that! If you need something, you call me!" She was upset with him and did not understand why he kept fooling with the chair. He'd never done that before.

"Then B brought the food in, and she and Dad started eating dinner together like they usually did. All of a sudden, for the third time, the lift chair starts going up, up . . . and up, standing my dad up all over again—right in front of B!" Can you imagine Beatrice's face as she saw this happening while sitting right there? As Jack tells the story, guffawing the entire time, anyone would realize this scene could have been in a movie. Actually, this scene should be in a movie.

Listeners to Jack's story have to wait while he quits laughing to hear to hear the end. Finally he finished this strange story. "It turned out Dad's lift chair had a short in it." Even telling the end of the story starts Jack laughing all over again, although the story happened 20 years ago.

When B told Jack what had happened with his dad and the chair, she ashamedly admitted, "Oh, Mr. Jack, I feel so bad. I feel *so* bad. I raised my voice. I just chewed your dad out talkin' so loud and nasty to him to quit it." Jack chuckled and "doubts seriously B's 'nasty' was much."

He continued, "The problem was, at that point, my dad couldn't talk or move on his own, so he couldn't explain to B that he hadn't done anything with the remote to make the chair move." Jack loves to remember this bizarre story, picturing his dad hangin' on for dear life in the tilted lift chair, picturing B, and the confusion of that whole scene. Once again, events from seemingly slow, routine days can make the very best stories. B told me this story once and got so tickled, I couldn't even understand the ending of the story.

Todd also had a story about B and Mr. Brown. "One day Mr. Brown had passed out with a seizure. Grandmama began hitting him and like to beat him to death."

"Mr. Brown, Mr. Brown, wake up! You aren't gonna die on me! No you aren't! Wake up! You can die on Alverna, but you are not gonna die on me!"

"Grandmama was scared and let him have it. She was not gonna lose him." Mr. Brown's seizure was soon over.

Beatrice loved Mr. Brown and was sad when he died. She told me she would miss him but said, "I will not miss Diamond."

Jack's assistant inherited Diamond after his dad's death, and Diamond found happiness once away from Beatrice. The cat was often seen sitting proudly in the front seat of the assistant's convertible. Jack still laughs at this turn of events for Diamond, the cat, and still wishes he'd had a chance to tell B of Diamond's new home and status because "for sure, there would have been a B response."

27

The Professor and the Nurse

B eatrice viewed death as much a part of life as living. In her work, she had seen death many times, even the tiny baby in the E.R. at Parkland but mostly elderly men and women she cared for. What I finally realized is that when one of B's patients died, not only did she have to say goodbye to someone she cared about but also goodbye to a job and paycheck. Even with gaps of financial insecurity, her faith prevailed. She once told me, "The good Lord has always taken care of me gettin' work."

Beatrice's employment in caregiving had always been from referrals. An example of this was my mother who was seeking a nurse to care for me after back surgery. She called my friend, Julie, who recommended Beatrice.

B always chuckled and told the story of Mother calling her. "Your mother told me she was looking for a nurse for her daughter, but she first wanted to interview me and asked if we could meet at El Fenix at Northpark for lunch. I told her 'I'll be glad to meet you there.' Your mother called back in a couple of days and said, 'Beatrice, that won't be necessary.' She gave me the date and time of your surgery." B was tickled at Mom because she'd never been asked for a private interview before. She'd never used an employment agency. She always had work by word of mouth from those who'd been fortunate enough to have her involved in their lives.

B was not offended that my mother wanted to interview her. That was fine with her. Some nurses might have been offended, but B seemed to always accept the differences in people. As Beatrice got to know how cautious my mother was through years of being with her, she'd recall those two phone calls from Mom and chuckle all over again.

Mr. Brown died just about the time my mother transitioned from assisted living to needing 24-hour care, so B began working every day for Mom without any gap in work. When my mother died in 2009, there was a short gap when B didn't have work. She was 79 years old and anxious to get another job.

B and I talked frequently by phone after Mother's death. We hadn't gone more than a day or two in over eight years without talking, even if a brief, "B, how's Mom today" on the phone. Now when we chatted, B would always ask, "Well, have you found me a job?"

"No, I haven't."

"Why not?" We'd both laugh. So many times one did not have an answer for Beatrice. It wasn't my place to get her a job, and she and I both knew that, although I was alert for any friend who needed help for an elderly parent or themselves. But the way B would ask sounded as if it were my job. At the end of our conversation, I knew what was coming. "Okay now, go find me a job." I would smile and say goodbye. I guess the good Lord was finding work for B, but she was sure doing her part.

One day a friend did call and asked if I knew if Beatrice was available and if she might like a job. Praise God! I could now resign from being an employment agency and being prodded by B about a job. "Yes, Fran, she is available." I explained my enthusiasm and gave her B's phone number. B was at work the next day, this time caring for a retired professor.

Dr. Donald Jackson was the father and father-in-law of two close friends, Don and Fran Jackson. He had been professor emeritus at the Perkins School of Theology. He taught sociology of religion. Dr.Jackson began teaching at Perkins in the 1950s, terribly divisive years for race relations in Dallas. If the 1950s were uncomfortably divisive, the '60s were visibly angry and often violent years in Dallas.

The first line of Dr. Jackson's obituary in *The Dallas Morning News* stated: "The Rev. Douglas E. Jackson worked to improve race relations in Dallas during his decades as a professor .... The award-winning professor also instructed Dallas police cadets about diversity and served on panels and commissions that advanced racial harmony."

Dr. Jackson's son, Don, described his father: "His life was hallmarked by his faith that directed all of his actions. He was constantly speaking out on issues where he felt society was straying from God's word."

A fellow professor said, "He [Dr. Jackson] was never afraid to speak his mind, even questioning Dallas's business leaders in a national magazine after the Kennedy assassination. He . . . told it very forthrightly. He was knowledgeable about the city."

Clarity of core beliefs and conviction of what real Christianity is guided Dr. Jackson's actions. Lack of fear to speak his beliefs in a divided and conservative city took courage. People listened to this soft-spoken man.

This was exactly like Beatrice. She was crystal clear in her Christian beliefs, able to withstand criticism, and always moving forward. She might have listened to or ignored criticism, but she did not fear it. B and Dr. Jackson, unacquainted at the time, represented examples in their communities that were sorely needed in the 1950s and 60s. One was not in the public eye at all; one was very much in the public eye. One was at home with five children and working in a nursing home; one taught at a leading university and was a proactive leader in Dallas during civil rights days. So different, yet both took a stand from the platforms each had when and where it mattered.

Beatrice, N.D., and their five small children lived in the midst of volatile racial division between Dallas's conservative social and political base and angry blacks demanding equality after years of Jim Crow laws. Tensions were high. How difficult it must have been to raise a family in this angry social culture with a daily threat of violence and rioting. Yet unknown to Beatrice, Dr. Jackson and other Dallas leaders were advocating for her black race during these angry and difficult days. Dr. Jackson was working to make life better for Beatrice and her family half a century before she even knew him.

The years in which Dr. Jackson was active and outspoken on racial issues that plagued Dallas were the very years Beatrice was raising children. There was anger before the Civil Rights Law was passed and after the bill passed. Sending children to school during the implementation of school integration was difficult for both black and white parents. As a mother of children who were often targets at school from angry white students, B had to not only teach but also be an example to her children of how to honorably respond to often cruel and unjust treatment. Beatrice Jones could not have known that she was indirectly being helped by Dr. Jackson, the very man she would one day help.

Because Fran was the most available family member to check on Dr. Jackson, she was the source of interesting and funny stories of B and her father-in-law. Although Dr. Jackson had lost his ability to get around, his mind stayed razor sharp as he aged. His caregiver also had a mind that was razor sharp.

B and Dr. Jackson had "endless talks on politics, the church, theology, current events, why things happened, and history of early denominations. Beatrice was endlessly curious and thrilled to talk to a professor. She was smart and wise and soaked up new information like a sponge." These two different yet both thinking individuals had all day long to talk, and talk they did. The common base from which they both lived and spoke was an unshakable Christian faith.

Another crossover between the lives of Beatrice and Dr. Jackson was Todd, B's grandson. At the time B worked for Dr. Jackson, Todd was enrolled at Perkins Theological School. B talked a lot about Todd and his education to Dr. Jackson. "They had long conversations about what Todd was learning and what he'd read. Beatrice wanted to understand what it meant to be ordained." Dr. Jackson was a teacher extraordinaire; B, his student. B was a nurse extraordinaire; Dr. Jackson, her patient.

I hope Dr. Jackson shared the following story with B. I wonder if Todd knows the story. The first group of black students who graduated from Perkins had been admitted unofficially since they were black. These five young men had to be taught off-campus, and Dr. Jackson was one of the professors who taught them. Their grades were kept by a secretary in a shoe-box under her bed. Could this have jeopardized Dr. Jackson's career? I do not know the answer to that. I do know his actions were courageous—especially in Dallas in the 1950s and '60s. I know Beatrice's responses of not feeling sorry for her children and teaching them how to respond to injustice, in addition to taking a stand at Titche's and the barbecue shack, were also courageous—especially in Dallas in the 1950s and 1960s.

Dr. Jackson and B had a common acquaintance, Zan Holmes. Zan was in the second group of black students to graduate from Perkins. "He was active in the Civil Rights Movement in Dallas. . . . Zan is a pillar of the Methodist denomination and has served on city boards. Beatrice knows Zan Holmes well. Each time B would see Dr. Holmes, he would ask, 'How are our people?'" "Our people" meant Dr. Jackson and his family. Reverend Zan Holmes, Beatrice's friend and Dr. Jackson's student, conducted Dr. Jackson's funeral service. Beatrice sat with the Jackson family to say goodbye to a good friend.

The parts of Beatrice's and Dr. Jackson's pasts that overlapped are fascinating. Common threads of their lives bound these two individuals together, but they didn't know this until half a century later. They had not known each other as their lives unknowingly intertwined. B's friendship with Dr. Jackson is another beautiful part of Beatrice's life story. Their time together was an ending for both—Dr. Jackson's life and Beatrice's career. Was this a miracle friendship that God brought together at just the right time? It surely seems so.

The story Fran loves best reflects the gentle nature of Dr. Jackson and the direct nature of Beatrice. Dr. Jackson was diabetic as was Beatrice, another common bond. Just as Jack gets so tickled as he tells his B and Mr. Brown "classic," Fran still chuckles aloud as she tells a B and Dr. Jackson classic.

"DeeDee [Dr. Jackson] was usually on a great diet since he

was diabetic, but he had such a longing for sweets that would occasionally burst out. B was the only one who'd hold the line with him and not let him persuade her for something sweet." Dr. Jackson was brilliant yet humble and soft-spoken. It would have been hard to refuse a simple request from this kind, elderly man. He even made his request a clever nonrequest.

On this particular day after lunch, B asked Dr. Jackson, "How'd you enjoy your lunch?"

"My lunch was wonderful—I believe I'll have some ice cream."

Quick as a wink, he heard, "I believe you won't. Would you like some apple?" Request made, request denied. From the kitchen, Dr. Jackson clearly heard Beatrice's response to his cleverly worded request, and just as my mother had no answers for B's logic, neither did Professor Jackson.

B had been cleaning up lunch dishes when Dr. Jackson stated his wish for ice cream, but she didn't take the bait of a polite request even from a kind, elderly man who rarely made requests. Diabetics don't eat ice cream. Period. Beatrice was the boss. Not even a professor emeritus from Perkins School of Theology who had stood up to the conservative base of Dallas could change that fact.

Beatrice's short time with Dr. Jackson was her last job after nursing and caring for the sick and elderly for over 60 years. Retiring in one's 80s? No surprise if you know Beatrice Jones. Dr. Jackson lived less than two years after B began caring for him. A year later, she herself began not feeling well.

28

January 1, 2009

In mid-December 2008, we decided to move my mother into a nursing home. Her finances were being depleted, and she had nursing home insurance. She was becoming weaker by the day, and her death was imminent. My brother and I wanted to make sure there would be enough money for Beatrice to stay with Mom because B was depending on a job, and my mother was depending on B. With B and Mom still a team, stress for this transition would be lessened. At this point, I did not know if my mother was even aware of moving.

As I look back on that cold December morning when B put Mother in her wheelchair to take her to my car, we paused for the last time at the door of her apartment and looked back. How many memories and stories there'd been in these few rooms with Mom and B. Mother looked around; there were two movers who were unaware they were dismantling her home, and all too quickly, pictures and dishes were packed in boxes, the rooms almost empty.

My mother's brown eyes slowly scanned the living room. I was sad. Did she understand? I hadn't thought she would understand, but at that moment, there's no doubt in my mind she knew she was saying goodbye to more than her apartment. She knew. I know she knew. I should have talked to her about the move even if she hadn't fully understood. I regret that even today.

Before the three of us walked out of the apartment where the summer day we had moved in, Mom looked around the room, from the same spot she sat now, and slowly said as she kept looking, "Mary, this looks like home." Mom was now leaving what had been home in the last years of her life. I kept my emotions at bay because I had a job to do. B transferred Mom into my car and fastened her seat belt. It was a cold and gray December day, but she was warm in her red fleece Christmas robe. We drove away from the apartment for the very last time. I drove slowly, not wanting to arrive at the nursing home. Beatrice followed.

Mother's belongings had been pared down to only a chest, TV, and her blue chair. Movers brought these to the Traymore. The blue chair was the most important. The sofa and lamps, the happy yellow and blue drapes that had matched her blue chair in the bedroom, her piano, her mother's dining room table, and other furniture, B's youngest son, Rickey, came to get. There was no more use for these things that had been part of Mom's home.

Mom and I drove a few blocks with only soft Christmas music on the radio. The warmth in the car and carols that played softly in the background created a never-to-be-forgotten intimacy. Neither of us spoke until Mother made a quiet observation, "This is a nice car." No smile. I looked at her and placed my hand in hers, and with no words spoken, that's how we drove for 20 minutes until we reached the Traymore.

The still silence spoke the deep love of a mother and daughter. The silence spoke the fact that, after 15 years of taking Mom places, this was the last time we would ever drive together. I knew, she knew. B was behind us, and that was reassuring. That bittersweet drive in my car is a memory I've never spoken of before because it was too sweet and precious to share.

The weeks of December became harder. Beatrice was there when hospice came in. To let go is hard, even when it is right to do so. Beatrice Jones had experienced deep pain and loss but saw death as God's infinite and loving plan for our lives. She also understood the pain of loss.

Beatrice was there almost every day. If she wasn't, Vera came. Some days Mother would sit in her blue chair. After Christmas, Mother was too weak to open her eyes, but I could see her closed eyes blink. Voices were quieter. There was no more laughter. I would sit by my mother's bed holding her hand and saying goodbye. I'd talk about childhood memories; what a wonderful, strong, and incredible mother she'd been; and how much she was loved—just as I'd seen her do with her own mother as she lay dying.

I wasn't even aware of Beatrice yet knew she was there. She heard and saw everything, and it was so right the three of us were together. B's presence was comforting. She would quietly leave to go home at night and be back in the morning. Beatrice was there on New Year's Day, the morning my mother breathed her last.

I'd accepted an invitation to a New Year's Eve dinner party with good friends. It was a wonderful evening of games, food, and light-heartedness, even with a heavy heart. Then I slept. On New Year's Day, I was dressed, with keys in hand, to go see my mother when the phone rang. The nurse at the Traymore told me my mother would not last another hour and to come now. How could I be stunned? But I was. I knew this was her time, but it was New Year's Day. Do people really die on New Year's Day? What a strange thing to think. My mother had survived so many illnesses she shouldn't have but not this time.

I was five minutes away when my phone rang. "Your mother is gone." I hung up and hit the steering wheel hard with my fist, wondering why God couldn't have waited five more minutes to take her. Five minutes. I should have been there. B was there.

I walked in, saw my mother lying still and peaceful, as if asleep, with eyes closed but no blinking. She was gone. Finally the tears fell. I fell into Beatrice's arms sobbing. It was New Year's Day, and B was working. She'd been my right arm for years. At that moment, she was my strength.

Death is a part of life. I didn't like it. I was relieved. I hated this day. I was relieved. How could I be feeling two such opposite emotions? Beatrice's calmness and compassion made this unreal setting seem natural. B was there for me. She had been there for me. She had been there for Mother. Beatrice Jones had been my mother's loyal companion at the very end.

B described the morning for me. "I walked in, and your mother's face looked so peaceful. I asked her if she wanted something to eat. She took a couple of bites of yogurt. I began to gently bathe her. I started at her feet and saw the purple around her toenails. I knew then it would be soon. I kept slowly bathing her. She always liked her bed bath. Mary, she was so at peace. Soon her breathing slowed. Then her breathing stopped. She left peacefully—and that's often not the way it is. Her face from early in the morning till her last breath was peaceful. Her breathing was so natural as she just went to sleep. Mary, that is what you need to know." B had sat by my mother's bed holding her hand as she passed from one life to the next. My mother died holding the hand of her trusted and best friend.

B knew I needed to know this. The sweetness and peace of Mother's last hours comforted me. Hospice had asked me a few days before if I was a Christian. Yes. This dear nurse said to me, "You need to know when your mother breathes her last, my belief is that Jesus will already have her hand in His hand and walk her from her earthly home to her heavenly home." I was desperate for comfort in my grief, and this sweet picture gave me that comfort.

It took a month after the death of my mother to wonder why Beatrice hadn't called me that morning instead of the nurse, so I could have been with Mom when she died. Shouldn't I have been? To not wonder that until now shows how much I trusted B with my mother. I hadn't even wondered until now. B intuitively understood the peaceful beauty on Mother's face and the quiet in the room. Her focus had been 110 percent on my mother, no one else.

I talked to a good friend later about B not calling me that morning. Debbie listened and paused, "Mary, wasn't your mother a very private person?"

"Yes."

"Mary, I don't think your mother wanted you there. I think she knew Beatrice could handle this day and knew being there would hurt you. She was with the person she wanted to be with when she died." I think my friend had an understanding of my mother that I was too close to see.

My presence would have disturbed the spiritual peace

and quiet of Mother's passing from this life to another where she would have no pain, perfect health, love, and joy—and a piano. It was right that Beatrice Jones was my mother's last human contact on this earth—that the warmth of the hand enfolding hers belonged to B. Maybe, just maybe, God's timing is perfect.

29

A Long Goodbye

I checked on B periodically after she retired. She was definitely slowing down but doing all right and was worried about not being able to afford a new washing machine. I told her I was scheduled for foot surgery and would be fine at home, but as I was saying this realized I might help us both out by hiring B once again. She could get help with a new washing machine, and I could get some assistance for a couple of days.

The afternoon after my surgery, Rickey, B's son brought her over. They rang the doorbell, and I step-clomped, step-clomped to the door. Beatrice chuckled at me and my boot, and I returned to bed knowing she knew her way around.

A few minutes later, B came into my room and sat in the comfortable chair by the window. This wasn't quite like old times because B was sitting. We chatted, and soon I told her I was too tired to talk anymore. I wanted to nap. She was supposed to get up and go in the other room but instead said, "Okay. Take a nap."

"B, I can't go to sleep with you sitting there looking at me."

"Sure, you can. Just go to sleep."

"I can't. Not when you're watching me."

"You won't see me watching you if you close your eyes. Take your nap."

No point arguing with B, and I'd never say, "B, please go in the other room" to this woman who simply wanted to sit in my chair. Beatrice Jones was tired, not from this day but from over half a century of nursing the sick. Life tired. I closed my eyes knowing I wouldn't be able to sleep and woke up two hours later with B still sitting there.

Later that evening, we said goodnight and agreed I'd call her if I needed help in the night. About 3:30 a.m., I called for B and got no response except loud snoring from the guest room. I called again, louder. The old B would have heard me. The aging B didn't. During those two days, I saw what I knew but hadn't wanted to see. The Beatrice I never thought could age was aging. Her health continued to decline in the next 18 months.

All too fast, Beatrice had traded places. Once the nurse, she was now the patient. She was 82 years old with a body fighting diabetes, high blood pressure, heart disease, and now old age. She slept much of the day and needed assistance walking, getting out of bed or a chair, showering, and dressing. She didn't talk much anymore, and her full-of-life joy had faded. Yet Beatrice's heart was still full of gratitude for kindnesses extended to her. As Marvella helped her out of the blue chair or out of bed, she would look right at her daughter and say, "Thank you."

When I visited B on her 84th birthday with a cake and flowers, I was totally surprised to hear her full wonderful laugh as she looked at me and said, "You crazy." That comment was the best thank you ever. I'd heard that from her before, and we chuckled together as we always had.

Three years later, B was helped to the blue chair, fed her meals, and was quiet, but her big, brown eyes saw everything. I'd taken the pictures of B and Mom in the red convertible and put them in a double frame as a gift for her. B surprised both Marvella and me with recognition of that priceless day in the red convertible, and we heard her joyful laugh once again.

I also gave her a bound, unproofed copy of my manuscript, which was in process of being edited for the publisher. I doubt B understood that one day there would be a book published about her, but I had an emotional need to place the manuscript in her hands. My purpose in writing had been to create a tribute to this incredible and unique woman I loved and respected. After staying too long visiting with B and Marvella, I gathered my things and prepared to leave. Unexpectedly B's head slowly turned, and she lifted her left hand and placed it on my arm, just as my mother had placed her hand on B's arm. Looking right at me, Beatrice quietly said, "Don't go." I looked at her and felt her love for me. I stayed.

B's health kept declining. The next year, she did not feel like company on her birthday or even hearing "Happy Birthday" on the phone. The doctor had told the family that Beatrice was in her "last stages." I don't guess he knew her very well at all. Just like my mother's "six more months," B's "last stages," too, turned into several years.

The tough B still hung in there without complaint. Her body was weak but her spirit strong. Beatrice Jones accepted life on life's terms and always had. This trait of her strength remained. She didn't fight being an invalid; she continued living the best she could although having to be helped with every aspect of her life. The assurance her family had was that

B, at times, showed her spunk, saying things that made her family laugh—unexpected comments that no one else could have come up with except her.

On a fall day, Patrice came to visit her grandmother. Those two had been a tight pair ever since Patrice was a little girl. She was now a grandmother herself, which made Beatrice a great-great-grandmother. That day, dementia had taken over B's thinking but not all of it.

Patrice walked into her grandmama's room when she arrived and greeted B as she always had: "Hi, Grandmama."

"Hi, Sal."

"Grandmama, it's Patrice, your granddaughter."

"Not today. You're Sal today!" Patrice, surely, was hurt at first but came to smile and appreciate the spirit of B's comment. Her grandmama might be in bed, but she was still Grandmama. Beatrice will always be that unique Mama, Grandmama, Beatrice, Be-At, or B even if we can't see her. The mold for Beatrice Dilworth Jones was broken with her arrival on April 9, 1930.

Holidays. Everybody, the whole family—B's children, grandchildren, great- and great-great-grandchildren, nieces, and nephews—still gathered as they always had, now at Marvella's. In her late 80s and in the winter of her life, Beatrice needed peace and quiet, not the noise of a crowd.

Vera recalled these holidays with laughter and kids running all over the place. To regain her needed quiet, the recognizable matriarch's orders were issued to the rambunctious children from her blue chair. "Go play somewhere else. Don't make me get outta this chair and whip everybody's ass." Vera got so tickled, as she always had, at the mama she loved.

On her last birthday, Rickey came to see his mother. Rickey was the one who'd always picked B up from work if she didn't have her car. They visited. She was quiet but alert, and as Rickey said goodbye to his mother, Beatrice looked squarely at him and began singing in a small voice, "Hap-py birth-day. . . to you. . . ." Then she said, "I have your back." Marvella, laughing, said she'd never heard her mother say "I have your back" and didn't think she knew what it meant, but we were talking about Beatrice. Somehow she knew. Those times were loved by her family. Beatrice Jones lived what she believed: "God has a plan for us." I never ever saw her question that.

The news was on one night when the real Beatrice emerged and surprised Marvella and her husband. Tennell had been reelected to the Dallas City Council, and he was occasionally on television during the local news. That particular night, Tennell was on TV. Out of the blue, B turned to Tennell and said in her softer, quakier, but in-charge voice, "If I see your big head on that TV one more time, I'm gonna get up and pop it."

Beatrice Jones did not let go easily of those she deeply loved—her children and her family. I believe when she spoke those "B" comments, they were gifts to her children and family.

For 88 years, Beatrice Jones's pluck, loyalty, responsibility, work ethic, compassion, and love touched and impacted her children, grandchildren, great-grandchildren, great-great-grandchildren, parents, siblings, nieces, nephews, cousins, patients, patients' families, neighbors, members of Salem Baptist, coworkers, and so many others. Beatrice's sphere of influence went beyond those she knew. The server at Titche's, the servers at the barbecue shack in Clarksville, and so many with whom she had come in contact learned to respect this black woman who proudly represented her race.

Was Beatrice afraid of dying and death? Anyone who knew her would laugh at that thought. B's faith and certainty in God's plan had kept her from ever being afraid of death. I remember, once again, the words she spoke to me, years ago, when a tiny baby died: "Mary, we all have an appointed time. None of us is here to stay. Get that in your head. And if you've got a nice place to move to, you don't mind moving. No problems there. We've made so much out of dying, and we've never done it, so we don't know. . . . Mary, if it's gonna be for me to have a bad stroke, then that's what I'll die from. We don't know what it'll be. The Lord is with me."

B could talk about death as easily as a grocery list. That was because she saw death as simply a part of life. If one is living, he or she will die. Beatrice's faith in God's plan and timing was rock solid. She helped others not to fear her death or theirs.

Vera reminded me what Beatrice had told her children over the years when she'd been hospitalized, and I couldn't keep myself from bursting out laughing when I heard this because I could literally hear B saying these exact words. Vera recalled her mother's admonition: "When God calls me home, don't be actin' like fools, cryin' and falling all over me, and screamin' and all that stuff. Just let me go."

I knew the "cryin'" would happen because of the time B had been hospitalized while working for my mother, and her large family descended on the hospital to be with her. Her heart problem had flared up, and she'd been hospitalized. I drove down to Baylor Hospital one evening to see her. When I tapped and opened the door, I saw at least 15 adults and children. I couldn't believe all the family that was there. They were there to stay and see that Beatrice was taken care of. I was envious.

I chuckled as I realized Beatrice's room wasn't a regular hospital room. Her room was huge, the largest hospital room I'd ever seen. B, in the bed, looked like a queen with her subjects all around. If B had this kind of response from her family when this wasn't a critical situation, I saw what it would be like when "God called her home." I couldn't imagine the intensity of emotion that would occur. Beatrice's family adored her. She was stability. She was the rock of the family. She loved deeply but was not outwardly emotional like her family.

After a few minutes, I took her hand and said goodbye. B said to me, with subdued noise of adults, teenagers, and children in this large room, "Get these people outta here." I smiled, shrugged my shoulders, and waved bye.

Later I asked Marvella how in the world her mother ended up in that huge hospital suite. One word: "Tennell." Of course—Tennell—our city councilman and mayor pro tem who knew who to call to get the largest suite he could for Beatrice. Tennell loved and took care of his mother-in-law the way he knew how, just as Marvella, Todd, Tyler, Vera, Rickey and the rest of the family took care of Beatrice.

Every time thoughts and memories of Beatrice cascade into our hearts, she is with us. Every time we think of the wise or funny things she'd say, she is with us. Every time life is hard and we hear, "Just hold your head high. You know who you are. Keep moving forward," or "Just let it go," or "Quit your cryin'," she is with us.

Beatrice's words come back to me: "You might as well get ready because people are gonna die. I know my heart is right, so I'm not worried. When I go in that ground, I won't know it because I'll be dead. I came in this world alone, and I'll leave alone."

Beatrice and I addressed her own death, specifically. One day I had stopped to visit with Mother, and she was resting. Aware of her continual declining health in her late 90s, I had my mother's death was on my mind, and I went in to talk to B. As she was putting clothes in the washing machine, I looked at her and mandated to Beatrice Jones, "B, you better not ever die!" She put the clothes down and turned around to face me.

"Well, I'm gonna. So you better wish for something else."

"Okay then, I'm going to get up and speak at your funeral."

"You do that, and I'll get up outta that casket and snatch you bald!'

"Why, B?"

"Because people get up there at funerals and talk about so-and-so and how sweet and wonderful she was, and she was probably the meanest woman you'd ever seen. They do that all the time. If you have something nice to say to me, say it while I'm alive." That is one of the wisest pieces of advice I have ever received.

"All right, B. I'll come put flowers on your grave."

"Well, if you do, just walk on by and kick a little dirt because, you know, it's 'dust to dust, ashes to ashes . . .' and you . . . you just keep a steppin.'"

More About Beatrice's
Life and Times

Boessenecker, John. *Texas Ranger: The Epic Life of Frank Hamer, the Man Who Killed Bonnie and Clyde.* Thomas Dunne, 2016.

Boston, Talmage. *Baseball and the Baby Boomer: A History, Commentary, and Memoir.* Bright Sky, 2009.

McElroy, Njoki PhD. *1012 Natchez.* Brown Books, 2009.

Robinson, Jackie. *An Autobiography of Jackie Robinson: I Never Had It Made.* HarperCollins. 1972.

Texas State Historical Society. *Handbook of Texas Online.*

Texas State Historical Society. *Handbook of African American Texas.* 2013.

Uhry, Alfred. *Driving Miss Daisy.* Theatre Publication, 1993.

Washington, Denzel, dir. *The Great Debaters.* 2007, Movie.

About the Author

Mary Harris loves storytelling, especially humorous vignettes about relationships. She specializes in flash fiction with a quirky eye on human behavior. She's written about why God would ever allow a speeding ticket on the way to church, her dream of Matlock and Judge Judy as her lawyer and judge when she was unexpectedly sued, or the life-impacting loss of a spelling bee in third grade.  Occasionally Mary is introspective such as remembering a lonely hike high in the Colorado Rockies. Whatever she writes, readers laugh or identify with as they remember their own experiences.

Former teacher, community volunteer, experienced world traveler, engaged mother, and adoring grandmother, Mary returned to college in her 60s and graduated with a Master of Liberal Studies degree in creative writing. She's consistently encouraged in her writing by a four-year-old grandson who loves trains and is observant and curious about everything, a ten-year-old granddaughter who takes her journal everywhere as she writes her own stories, and a one-year-old grandson who's afraid of nothing. Big Ben, Mary's wooly, two-year-old doodle, offers inspiration and support while lying at her feet as she writes—with a bone, of course.

Mary's experience managing her mother's care led to Beatrice Jones, a caregiver and best friend whose infectious laughter and practical wisdom echoed throughout the aging years for Mary and her mother. Raised in Houston, Mary lives and writes in Dallas, Texas, sharing her literary adventures with her Dark and Stormy Writers Group.

Stay tuned for more from Mary Elizabeth Harris.

To contact Mary and read some of her flash fiction, please visit www.beatricekeepasteppin.com

"I'm not concerned with your liking or disliking me . . . .
All I ask is that you respect me as a fellow human being."

JACKIE ROBINSON

"Keep a Steppin'"